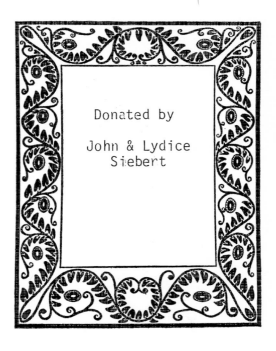

Donated by

John & Lydice
Siebert

HANDBOOK to the
NEW TESTAMENT

CLAUS WESTERMANN

Translated and Edited by
Robert H. Boyd

AUGSBURG PUBLISHING HOUSE
Minneapolis **Minnesota**

This volume is a translation of the introduction and New Testament sections of *Abriss der Bibelkunde* published in 1962 by Verlagsgemeinschaft Burckhardthaus- und Kreuz-Verlag GmbH. (4th edition, 1966), Stuttgart/Gelnhausen, Germany.

Scripture quotations are from the Revised Standard Version of the Bible, copyright 1946 and 1952 by the Division of Christian Education of the National Council of Churches.

Translator's Preface

St. Augustine's ancient dictum that "the Old Testament is implicit in the New, the New Testament becomes explicit in the Old" has sometimes been interpreted so as to make the Testaments virtually identical in message and purpose. This is clearly not the case in this handbook to the New Testament, which now in its English translation completes the survey of the Bible undertaken by Claus Westermann in his *Abriss der Bibelkunde (Handbücherei des Christen in der Welt, Band 1)*. The Old Testament section of this simple, clear, yet comprehensive biblical overview appeared in 1967 under the title *Handbook to the Old Testament*.

In his introduction Professor Westermann states: "From beginning to end the Bible gives an account of a great history, diverse and manifest, focused in the account concerning Jesus of Nazareth. Individual biblical words can only be rightly perceived in connection with this account and in relation to its central message." The Christocentric character of the biblical message could only be adumbrated in the Old Testament portion of this vast survey. It is in this New Testament section that it becomes clearly evident, something that the author makes abundantly manifest as he expertly leads the reader through the books of the New Testament with frequent flashes of perceptive insight, demonstrating how they not only allude to the Old Testament but build upon its concepts. Thus one comes to appreciate how the cluster of events concerning Jesus Christ in the New Testament is linked with the history of Israel into whose midst he was born. His advent was "the fulfillment of the history of this nation and thereby the fulfillment of the history of the Old Testament."

This handbook, as the author suggests, is only intended to provide "the initial steps into the Bible," to be a guide in helping the student read the New Testament in relation to the Old on his own in a more perceptive fashion. It is not meant to be a complete digest of information about the New Testament. The many charts, outlines, and interpretive comments with which readers of the Old Testament handbook are familiar are provided as an aid in leading them into the world of the New Testament.

The format of the charts as they appear in the German original have been closely followed except in the case of the chart on 2 Timothy, which has been rearranged for the sake of greater clarity. Editorial changes and additions have been kept at a minimum and consist primarily of headings that have been added to individual sections to keep them in conformity with the charts and to maintain the outline form that has been adopted for the biblical books with the accompanying relevant interpretive comments. The scheme of notation and intention follows that recommended by *A Manual of Style* (The University of Chicago Press, 1949). It has been necessary therefore to disregard letters and numbers occasionally used in the German original.

When Scripture is quoted the Revised Standard Version has normally been followed, unless the comments of the author are based on a German version, conveying a different sense than that expressed in the English. In such cases, footnotes call attention to the difference between the English and German versions in relation to the original text.

I wish to express appreciation to Dr. Henry S. Gehman, Professor Emeritus of Princeton Theological Seminary, for helpful suggestions in the course of this translation and to my wife for her encouragement and assistance in much typing.

Luther Theological Seminary   ROBERT H. BOYD
St. Paul, Minn.

From the Author's FOREWORD

The essential material for this project has grown out of a course in Bible content that I conducted at the Kirchliche Hochschule in Berlin in the years following 1950. In my association with the students in this course I came to realize how important a basic knowledge of the Bible is for theological study as well as all subsequent church work. This book is intended for all who are convinced that a survey of the entire Bible is a necessary prerequisite for a responsible communication of the words of Scripture in preaching, teaching, and the practical ministry. . . . *

I am grateful to Dr. Dieter Georgi for many valuable suggestions in our work together on the New Testament.

---

*Translator's Note: English sources that provide a bibliography for the individual biblical books, and that correspond to German sources, cited here by the author are *The New Schaff-Herzog Encyclopedia of Religious Knowledge* (Supplementary volumes) (Grand Rapids, Mich.: Baker Book House, 1955) and *The Interpreter's Dictionary of the Bible* (New York: Abingdon Press, 1962).

Contents

Charts and Tables

A Time Chart*

OF SIGNIFICANT DATES IN THE HISTORY OF NEW TESTAMENT TIMES

Political History	Church History	New Testament Writings
Augustus (30 B.C.-A.D. 14)		
Herod the Great (40 B.C.-A.D. 4)		
Judea under Procurators (A.D. 6 ff.)		
Tiberius (14-37)		
Pontius Pilate (26-36)	John the Baptist (28-29)	
	Death of Jesus (30) (14 Nisan = 7 April)	
	Conversion of Paul (33) Journey to Arabia	
Caligula (37-41)	Paul in Jerusalem (ca. 35) (14 yrs. in Syria & Cilicia = 1st missionary journey)	
Claudius (41-54)		
	Persecution in Jerusalem (43-44)	
	Death of James	
	Apostolic Council (49) 2nd missionary journey	
	Paul in Corinth (Gallio) (ca. 50-51)	
		1 Thess. (52 ff.)

*The dates in this chart are based on the chronology of H. Reller, in "Kirchengeschichte (Zeittafel)," *Evangelisches Kirchenlexikon*. Göttingen. 1958. Vol. ii, cols. 663-665. Dates for New Testament writings include modifications as noted by C. Westermann.

Nero (54-68)	Paul in Ephesus & Mace- donia = 3rd missionary journey (54-56)	*1 Cor.* (Spring 54)
		Portions of *2 Cor.* (54-55) Composition of book (after 96)
	Paul in Corinth (54-58)	
		Galatians (56)
	Paul as a prisoner in Jerusalem & Caesarea (58-61)	*Philippians* (Spring 55?)
	Paul in Rome (61-63)	*Romans* (58)
		Philemon, Colossians (also Ephes.?) (62-63)
	Stoning of James (Jesus' brother) (63?)	
	Burning of Rome (64) Persecution of Nero (Death of Peter?)	
	Judean revolt (66 ff.)	
Vespasian (69-79)		
	Destruction of Jerusalem (70)	*Gospel of Mark* (after 70)
Titus (79-81)		*Gospel of Matthew* (75-90)
Domitian (81-96)		*Gospel of Luke* (75-95)
	Persecution in Rome (95)	*Revelation* (after 90)
Trajan (98-117)		*Hebrews* (90-100)
		Acts (end of 1st century)
		Gospel of John (ca. 100)
		1 Peter (ca. 100)
		1 John, James (ca. 100)
	Persecution in Antioch Ignatius, martyr in Rome (ca. 110)	*Pastoral letters* (beginning of 2nd century)
	Letter of Trajan to Plinus against the Christians (111-113)	*2 Peter* (middle of 2nd century)
		Canon of New Testament (relatively closed before 200)

INTRODUCTION

The Bible as a Whole

The New Testament

THE BIBLE AS A WHOLE

In a first over-all view of the entire Bible, the Old Testament appears as a great expanse alongside the smaller expanse of the New Testament. Both are composed of many smaller areas, which (as in a map) exhibit sometimes independent regions, merging into larger unities. All the writings of the Old and New Testaments were once independent books, before they were combined into the present collections.

Just as one can view a map as a historical presentation, exhibited on a flat surface, so a biblical handbook (which can deal but superficially with the biblical writings) directs one constantly to the history, to which there is only an allusion in this cursory presentation of the sections and outlines of the account. For the Bible in its totality is essentially a great history. It is only in reference to this history that one can read the writings and books and parts of the Bible in their true context. Only thus can one get at their significance.

In Luther's translation of the Bible, the same primary division is used for the table of contents of both Old and New Testaments, viz., Historical Books, Didactic Books, and Prophetic Books. This division, however, is but a superficial synopsis; for the books that appear under these headings have a much more diverse character. This is evident when one examines them more carefully.

There is a group of narrative or informative books in the Old and New Testaments, which are the origin as well as the matrix of the entire collection. These are the Pentateuch and the Gospels respectively. The reader of the Bible should take careful note of this fundamental material in both Testaments and never forget that it is the Bible's proper manner of speech—it tells a story. That the Old Testament and the New Testament agree in this is by no means accidental. It is essential to both. Besides this, however, they have much in common: both tell how God's history with his people in the old as well as in the new covenant turned out. At the heart of both is the account concerning the divine saving act whereby the covenant was established.

Neither is a historical account in the modern sense of the term but is rather a witness or testimony to that for which the faith and confession to those who here speak is basic. Closely connected with this is the fact that there are several witnesses narrating the individual events of which the history in almost all the Pentateuch and Gospels is composed. What is more, these two, three, or four accounts (as the case may be) do not agree literally—something quite characteristic of first-hand reports.

The only difference between the Pentateuch and the Gospels lies in the fact that the Gospel's first-hand reports exist side-by-side in separate books, whereas those in the Pentateuch have been woven together into one general account. Only Deuteronomy has remained as a separate account alongside the others. Here the correspondence with the New Testament is so close that Deuteronomy (like the fourth Gospel in relation to the other Synoptics) occupies also a special position. It consists especially of longer addresses.

From here on the differences are greater than the similarities. In the New Testament the Gospels are followed by the Acts of the Apostles, a history after the main event, telling how the apostles of Jesus Christ fared in the world. In the Old Testament the Pentateuch is succeeded by the account of Israel's history from the Book of Joshua to 2 Kings. The ancient designation for this section is "the Former Prophets," a title that gives decisive significance to the prophets, appearing in the course of this history or to the word of God, issuing through them. The work of the Chronicler (1 and 2 Chronicles, Ezra, and Nehemiah), which comes next, did not belong to the historical books according to the ancient arrangement but to "the Writings," hence to the third part of the canon. This is due to the character of its historical presentation, which is essentially different. The real historical books of the Old Testament conclude with the exile.

In the New Testament the Acts of the Apostles is followed by the epistles; in the Old Testament the "Former Prophets," by the prophetic writings. They correspond also to one another in this, that they are both concerned with a message and with the office of a messenger. It was only by the word they proclaimed that God's work on behalf of his people was accomplished in the ministry of the apostles as well as the prophets. This ministry was carried on with the one as well as the other amid opposition and trouble, and it was accepted only by small groups of people. The difference in the content of their message, however, immediately strikes the eye: the apostles were messengers of good news—the Gospel; the prophets, messengers of judgment, for the most part. When the latter, however, had good news to bring, they pointed to the future, whereas the apostles in their message pointed back to that which had taken place.

According to the arrangement in Luther's Bible the Revelation to John is the only prophetic book in the third part of the New Testament, and it has therefore been classified with the prophetic books of the Old Testament. This no longer agrees with present understanding of prophecy; for Revelation is an apocalypse—hence a book dealing with the "last things." In this respect it does not correspond with the prophetic books but with Daniel, the second part of which is also an apocalypse.

THE NEW TESTAMENT

There is something basically new that begins in the New Testament as over against the Old Testament even in the way its content is presented. The New Testament is the witness concerning *one* saving message for all mankind, a message that proclaims the *one* individual—Jesus Christ.

Whereas the Old Testament gives an account of something that took place over a period embracing nearly a thousand years, the New Testament account is confined to a few decades. Whereas the Old Testament enlarges upon God's dealings with his people throughout this long period, so as to include all areas of individual and national life, the New Testament from beginning to end concentrates on the one subject that is to be preached within every area of individual and national life, declaring:

"There is salvation in no one else,
for there is no other name under heaven
given among men by which we must be saved" (Acts 4:12).

It is from the aspect of this concentration on one subject that the plan of the New Testament is also to be understood. Apart from the Revelation to John, it consists of only two large complex sections—the Gospels and the Epistles. The Acts of the Apostles is at the heart, linking the two together. With its account of Jesus' ascension (ch. 1), Acts follows directly upon the Gospels. The way of the message, opening with the Pentecost event (ch. 2), is then described in the succeeding chapters of Acts. The Epistles, which follow in the second large complex section of the New Testament, were written at places along the way.

The stories of the Ascension and Pentecost with which Acts begins have still a direct connection with the cluster of events toward which all four Gospels from the outset proceed, viz., the passion, death, and resurrection of Jesus. This sequence of events accordingly stands clearly and unequivocally at the heart of the New Testament, not only from the standpoint of its subject matter but also its structure. The four Gospels move toward this series of events; Acts and the Epistles proceed from it. This is indicated above all by the insertion of the first epistle. The theme of Romans in 1:16 f. expresses this message exactly.

These two complex sections of the New Testament, at the center of which stands so unequivocally the message of Jesus' suffering, death, and resurrection, are then followed by an allusion to the end of history in the Revelation to John. This is a real part of the message of the New Testament, as is already indicated in the clear and detailed references to the last things in the Gospels and the Epistles. The *one* message of the New Testament is thus brought into relationship with the historical epoch between the advent of Jesus Christ and his return at the consummation.

This is matched by the way in which this cluster of events at the heart of the New Testament is linked with the history that goes before. It does not come to such clear expression in its structure, however—namely, that throughout the entire New Testament, the advent, suffering, death, and resurrection of Jesus Christ are related to God's dealing with the nation into whose midst Jesus was born. His coming is the fulfillment of the history of this nation and thereby the fulfillment of that which was promised in the Old Testament. The introductory sections of all four Gospels mention this (see below, pp. 16, 36). The way in which the Old Testament, however, is continually quoted in the Gospels, Epistles, and Revelation likewise expresses this. It is the real theme of the Letter to the Hebrews.

The one message around which everything in the entire New Testament revolves is thus placed at the center of time. It stands, on the one hand, as the fulfillment of the history of the Old Testament; on the other hand, as the announcement of Christ's return at the end of time.

Part One

THE GOSPELS AND ACTS

I

The Synoptic Gospels

All four Gospels bring the good news that the Christ has come in Jesus of Nazareth. All four Gospels testify to the divine saving act that occurred in his coming, his suffering, death and resurrection. Each of these four witnesses has at the same time its own style and bears witness from its own standpoint. In the closing section, dealing with Jesus' death and resurrection, the testimony of all four Gospels becomes quite similar. Here the heart of the New Testament is once more revealed.

Apart from this final section, the Gospel of John differs from the other three (the Synoptic Gospels) primarily in the fact that it contains chiefly longer connected addresses. It is distinguished by an evident theological character to a much greater extent than the other three.

The first three Gospels, the Synoptics, have overall the same structure. Thus the last three chapters of all three deal with Jesus' suffering, death, and resurrection (Matt. 26–28; Mark 14–16; Luke 22–24). Here the conformity in general as well as in detail is the most pronounced. This section in all three Gospels is preceded by two other sections: the journey to Jerusalem and Jesus' final activity there.

In the large central section, which deals with Jesus' activity in Galilee, there are the greatest number of divergencies both as to the order of the account and in the way the material is presented. At the beginning of this central section, however, which is concerned with the start of Jesus' activity, the correspondence is again quite evident. Only Matthew and Luke furnish an account of Jesus' early life.

	Matthew	Mark	Luke
Jesus' early life	1- 2		1- 2
Jesus in Galilee	3-18	1- 9	3-18
The Road to Jerusalem	19-20	10	18-19
In Jerusalem	21-25	11-13	19-21
Jesus' Suffering, Death, and Resurrection	26-28	14-16	22-24

Jesus' Early Life

Matthew and Luke furnish the only account of Jesus' birth. In Matthew the genealogy of Jesus* precedes the account of the visit of the wise men and the flight to Egypt. In Luke the story of Jesus' early life is quite comprehensive. The birth of John and Jesus as well as the announcement concerning their births is told in great detail. In addition, there is a nativity account at the close. The psalms that occur in association with the events are significant.

Jesus in Galilee

All three alike start with the reference to John the Baptist and the baptism of Jesus, the Temptation, his appearance in Galilee, and the call of the first disciples. Then the important differences begin. They are occasioned by the fact that Matthew and Luke, over and above Mark, have adopted the so-called Q source,† a collection of Jesus' sayings. They have, however, worked it into their account in quite different ways. Matthew and Luke, moreover, both include much traditional material that is peculiarly their own. Mark has only a few unique passages.

In the case of Matthew, the collections of speeches are especially prominent: the Sermon on the Mount (chs. 5–7), the message concerning the commissioning of the apostles (ch. 10), the collection of parables (ch. 13). Luke has included an important body of speeches in the so-called "Lukan Travel Account" (9:51–18:14).

---

*In Luke the genealogy is given in 3:23 ff.

†Translator's Note: Q is the abbreviation used for the non-Marcan source of Matthew and Luke. It consists of narrative material and sayings of Jesus. The symbol is derived from the German term *Quelle*, "source." The order of Q is thought more likely to be preserved in Luke than in Matthew, although attempts to reconstruct its content remain tentative.

It is only at the end that the three Gospels again converge in connection with Peter's confession, the first two announcements of the Passion, and the Transfiguration.

The Road to Jerusalem

Common to all three Gospels at this point is the collection of utterances concerning marriage and riches. In between is the story of Jesus' blessing the children. Following is the third announcement of suffering.

In Jerusalem

The last section, prior to the Passion story, begins in a uniform way in all three Gospels with the account of Jesus' entrance into Jerusalem. It closes in all three with the "Synoptic apocalypse," the reference to the end of the world and the last judgment. In between is the account of the controversy with the Pharisees and Sadducees and the announcement of the destruction of the temple. This last section is remarkably unified in itself. All pericopes deal directly or indirectly with the proclamation of judgment, the dark background of the saving message. The Passion story terminates with this judgment.

Jesus' Suffering, Death, and Resurrection

It is possible to see the events and sayings of the Passion story in three groups. At the center of the first group is the Lord's Supper, which begins with the plot concerning Jesus' death and the anointing at Bethany, followed by the sayings and events connected with the Lord's Supper, and combined with the designation of the betrayer.

The transition to the second group of passages is provided by the account of the walk to Gethsemane and the prayer in the garden. This second group leads in a continuous account from Jesus' capture to his death.

The third group in all three Gospels contains the account of the empty grave plus the various Easter stories in Matthew and Luke.

THE EARLY LIFE OF JESUS

	Matthew		Luke
Genealogy of Jesus	1:1-17	The Prologue	1:1-14
His Birth	1:18-25	The Promise (concerning Jesus and John)	1:5-38
Wise Men from the East	2:1-12	Birth of the Baptist	1:39-80
Flight (to Egypt) and Return	2:13-23	The Birth of Jesus	2:1-40
		The Twelve-year-old	2:41-52

JESUS IN GALILEE

	Matt.	Mark	Luke
John the Baptist and Jesus' Baptism	3	1	3
The Temptation of Jesus	4	1	4
His Appearance in Galilee; His First Disciples	4	1	4 f.
The Sermon on the Mount (Sermon on the Plain)	5-7	—	6
Healings and Other Miracles	8-9	1-3	5
The Disciples	10	3	10
Parables	13	4	8
Peter's Confession; the Announcement of Suffering	16	8	9
Jesus' Transfiguration	17	9	9
Lukan Travel Account			10-18

JOURNEY TO JERUSALEM

Marriage, Children, Riches	19	10	18
The Third Announcement of Suffering	20	10	18

IN JERUSALEM

Jesus' Entrance Into Jerusalem	21	11	19
The Cleansing of the Temple	21	11	19
Against the Pharisees and Sadducees	22 f.	12	20
Announcement of the Destruction of the Temple	24	13	21
The Synoptic Apocalypse	24 f.	13	21

JESUS' SUFFERING, DEATH, AND RESURRECTION

	Matt.	Mark	Luke
From the Plot of Death to Gethsemane ...	26	14	22
From Jesus' Capture to His Death	26-27	14-15	22-23
The Empty Grave and Easter	28	16	24

The above outline may be expressed in chart form as follows:

II

The Gospel of Matthew

This Gospel originated in the Jewish-Christian community between 75 and 90 A.D. and was addressed to Jewish-Christian congregations. Although it does not itself designate an author, it has been ascribed to the apostle Matthew ever since the time of Papias.*

This Gospel is especially interested in the way faith in Christ is related to the Old Testament and to the ancient people of God. This is indicated at every point, e.g., in the many Old Testament quotations, the emphasis on the controversy with the representatives of Jewish learning, the many repeated honorary titles concerning Jesus as the Messiah, and the stress on his authoritative teaching. In Jesus' teaching the Old Testament law is fulfilled (cf. the Sermon on the Mount) just as in his activity as the Son of Man. With his return in glory the progress of the church together with world history will be achieved in judgment and in salvation. Until that time the Lord grants to his church the promise of his presence, the mandate to carry on mission activity, and the ordering of church life.

A. JESUS' EARLY LIFE (Matt. 1—2)

Jesus' coming within the history of God's people of the old covenant is firmly established by his genealogy (1:1-17). He comes from the royal family (as the son of David), yet the harlot Rahab (Joshua 2) and the Moabitess Ruth also belong to this genealogy.

*Translator's Note: Papias was a bishop of Hieropolis in Asia Minor in the first half of the second century A.D. Only fragments of his five-volume work, entitled *Interpretations of the Lord's Oracles,* are now extant; but they include legendary accounts on the origin of the Gospels of Matthew and Mark.

Isaiah 7:14 already had prophesied the virgin birth of Jesus (1:18-25). That his birth would bring about a great change not only for Israel but for the whole world as well is indicated by the story of the wise men from the East who came from a distance to pay homage to the new king. At the same time, however, the other basic theme begins already in the story of Jesus' early life, viz., that the way of the new king will be a way of suffering (cf. the flight to Egypt and the return, 2:13-23).

B. JESUS IN GALILEE (Matt. 3—18)

1. The beginning of Jesus' activity (3:1—4:25)

a. The baptism of Jesus (3:1-17)

John the Baptist, in whom the prophetic office of God's ancient people once more was revived, stands at the beginning of Jesus' activity. His one task was to point to the one in whom the fulfillment has come and to prepare the way for him by a preaching that calls for conversion (3:1-12). In addition, however, John was to show by baptizing Jesus that he was the Savior, destined by God, just as many prophets had had the commission of designating the divinely appointed king.

In the divine utterance at the time of Jesus' baptism (3:17) there is a reminder of the royal designation (Ps. 2:7) and the confirmation of the Servant of the Lord (Isa. 42:1). The humiliation of the Son of God begins with Jesus' placing himself through baptism in the line of sinners.

b. The temptation of Jesus (4:1-11)

The story of the temptation is in the same vein. Here Jesus, in obedience to the Father, refuses to be a messiah that would come in power and glory.

c. In Galilee (4:12-25)

In this way the ground is prepared for Jesus' appearance in Galilee, the beginning of which (4:12-25) is then told. He proclaims in the towns of Galilee the coming of God's kingdom, healing many sick people and calling his first disciples, Peter, Andrew, James, and John. Thereby the ancient promises are fulfilled: "The people who walked in darkness have seen a great light" (Isa. 9:1).

2. The Sermon on the Mount (5:1—7:29)

This is not a sermon in our sense of the term but a summary of Jesus' preaching, arranged in sections from different viewpoints. The individual sayings must be understood each on its own basis, even as they were also once spoken.

The Beatitudes at the beginning (5:3-12) are an encouraging promise of salvation, addressed to the poor, the miserable, the ones who suffer and are persecuted. They correspond to the cry of the Savior in 11:28: "Come to me, all who labor and are heavy laden . . . . " However, on those who accept this invitation Jesus bestows the honor of being the salt of the earth, the light of the world, the city set on a hill (5:13-16). The basis for this is provided by the antithetical statements in 5:21-48, which are introduced by the announcement of the new righteousness (5:17-20). They all begin with the comment: "You have heard that it was said to the men of old . . . but I say to you . . . . " Jesus here proclaims the possibility of a new, complete obedience, as an "example of what it means, when the kingdom of God breaks into the world, which is still under sin, death, and the devil." *

The realization of this new righteousness in everyday life, through the giving of alms (vv. 1-4), prayer (vv. 5-13, 9-13— "The Lord's Prayer"), forgiveness (vv. 14 f.), fasting (vv. 16-18), is the subject of 6:1—7:12. Corresponding to the salvation which the Beatitudes announce to the poor is the message concerning freedom from care (vv. 19-34, "the birds and the lilies") and the assurance of answered prayer (7:7-11).

Various admonitions and warnings (7:1-6, 12-23) that could be termed prescriptions concerning entrance into the kingdom of God conclude the collection. At the end is the parable about the building of a house.

3. The Messiah of action (8:1—9:38)

   a. Stories of healing and deliverance
      (1) A leper (8:1-4)
      (2) The centurion's servant (8:5-13)

---

* J. Jeremias, *The Sermon on the Mount* (Philadelphia: Fortress Press, 1963), p. 31.

(3) Peter's mother-in-law and other sick people (8:14-17)
(4) The stilling of the storm (8:23-27)
(5) Two Gadarene demoniacs (8:28-34)
(6) A paralytic: healing and forgiveness (9:1-8)
(7) The woman suffering from a hemorrhage and the daughter of Jairus (9:18-26)
(8) Two blind men and a dumb demoniac (9:27-34)

b. Miscellaneous stories on discipleship
(1) Would-be followers of Christ (8:18-22)
(2) The call of Matthew (9:9-13)
(3) The rejection of fasting (9:14-17)
(4) A summary of Jesus' activity (9:35-36)
(5) A prayer for the harvest (9:37-38)

In the healings Jesus reveals himself as the Servant of the Lord, of whom the Song in Second Isaiah declares: "Surely he has borne our sicknesses" * (Isa. 53:3). Jesus' healing message is for the whole man so as to include also the forgiveness of sins, as stated in 9:1-8. This message encounters simple, humble faith. Jesus asks the two blind men: "Do you believe I am able to do this?" Because they believe he is able to grant healing (likewise in 8:5-13; 9:18-26). The story of the calming of the tempest (8:23-27) also has to do with deliverance from deadly peril.

In addition to these miracle stories there is the account of the call of Matthew, the tax-collector (9:9-13), the story of the different men who wanted to follow Jesus (8:18-22), and Jesus' rejection of fasting on the part of the disciples (9:14-17), all of which have to do with discipleship (*Nachfolge*). At the end is a summary of Jesus' activity together with a prayer to the Lord of the harvest (9:35-38).

4. The commissioning of messengers (10:1-42)

a. The appointment of the twelve apostles (10:1-4)
b. Instruction for the messengers (10:5-16)
c. Warning against times of persecution (10:17-25)
d. Be not afraid! (10:26-39)
e. The honor of being messengers (10:40-42)

---

*Translator's Note: The rendering "sicknesses" follows here the marginal reading. The Hebrew original for this term is *ḥŏlāyēnû*, which means literally "our sicknesses," the rendering adopted also by the German.

Jesus required messengers for his work on earth. He appointed the twelve and sent them out with his commission, supreme authority, and promise. They were not only conveyors of his message (v. 7) but also bearers of his healing power (v. 8) and blessing (vv. 11-15, 40-42). Their mission was limited at first to Israel (vv. 5 f.). It was not necessary for them to be concerned about their own livelihood (vv. 9 f.) nor about what they were to say (v. 19). They are fully informed concerning the difficulty of their task—the persecutions and travail of the final age that awaited them (vv. 17-25), "but he who endures to the end will be saved" (v. 22). Even as the prophets were told not to fear (e.g. Jer. 1:17-19), so the followers of Jesus are reassured on their grim way. They will remain safe within the fatherly goodness of God (vv. 26-31). Their Lord will stand by them (vv. 32 f.). The final age will be the time of separation (vv. 34-36) and of wholehearted decision for or against Christ (vv. 37-39).

5. The question of John (11:1-30)

    a. The question of John and Jesus' answer (11:1-6)
    b. Jesus' comment concerning John the Baptist (11:7-19)
    c. Woes pronounced upon Chorazin, Bethsaida, and Capernaum (11:20-24)
    d. The call of the Savior (11:25-30)

After the activity of Christ has been described in word (chs. 5–7) and deed (chs. 8–9) and the messengers have been sent forth, the one who at the outset had declared: "This is the one!" asks: "Are you really the one?" As an answer Jesus points to his own words and works, but adds: "Blessed is he who takes no offense at me" (v. 6). After Jesus' comment concerning John, in which he also speaks positively of the one who thus questions him, the decisions for or against Jesus as the Son of God are contrasted in an utterance concerning judgment (vv. 20-24) and salvation (vv. 25-30).

6. The enmity of the Pharisees (12:1-50)

    a. Plucking ears of grain on the Sabbath (12:1-8)

b. Healing on the Sabbath (12:9-21)
c. Healing a deaf-mute and a speech against the Pharisees (12:22-37)
d. The Pharisees' demand for a sign (12:38-42)
e. The unclean spirit (12:43-45)
f. "My mother and my brothers!" (12:46-50)

The deeds and words of Jesus arouse the hostility of the religious legalists. He sets the graciousness of God (vv. 1-8) and the love for one's neighbor (vv. 9-21) over against the rigid observance of the Sabbath. He sets his supreme authority, in which God's kingdom is coming into being (v. 28), over against the charge that he is in league with Satan. This power is confirmed in the Scriptures. He is the Servant of the Lord (vv. 18-21), announced in Isaiah (42:1-4).

7. The parabolic discourse (13:1-58)
a. The sower (13:1-9). Interpretation (13:18-23)
b. The significance of the parables (13:10-17, 34-35)
c. Weeds among the wheat (13:24-30). The interpretation (13:36-43)
d. The mustard seed and the leaven (13:31-33)
e. The treasure in the field and the precious pearl (13:44-46)
f. The fish net. That which is old and new (13:47-52)
g. The prophet in his own country (13:53-58)

All the parables are concerned with the wonder of the breaking in of God's dominion. This dominion is hidden in the appearance of a man among men and in an apparently impotent message that seems at first to alter nothing as to the present world's stability. The parables thus speak of the beginning of God's sovereignty. The beginning is so many-sided, even as the parables themselves can be understood in varied ways. The beginning also takes place so definitely in this present world that it can be demonstrated in the simplest happenings of actual everyday life. The amazing feature about these parables lies in this very fact that they speak of God's decisive action in our world in a language that is in no way theological or sacred.

**8. From the execution of the Baptist to the announcements of
the Passion (14:1—18:35)**

   a. Miscellaneous accounts
- (1) The repudiation of Jesus in his home town (13:53-58)
- (2) The execution of the Baptist (14:1-12)
- (3) Peter's confession and the first prediction of the Passion (16:13-23)
- (4) The Transfiguration (17:1-13)
- (5) The second prediction of the Passion (17:22-23)

   b. Miracles and healings
- (1) Feeding of the five thousand (14:13-21). The four thousand (15:32-39)
- (2) Sinking Peter (14:22-33)
- (3) Healing of many sick people (14:34-36; 15:29-31)
- (4) Healing of the epileptic boy (The disciples' failure) (17:14-19)

   c. Controversial talks
- (1) The great transgression (15:1-9)
- (2) Clean and unclean (15:10-20)
- (3) The sign of Jonah (16:1-4)
- (4) The leaven of the Pharisees (16:5-12)

   d. The life of the church
- (1) Concerning discipleship (16:24-28)
- (2) The temple tax (17:24-27)
- (3) The dispute among the disciples over status (18:1-5)
- (4) Temptation (18:6-10)
- (5) Congregational discipline (18:15-20)

   e. Parables
- (1) The lost sheep (18:12-14)
- (2) The unfaithful servant (18:21-35)

In the midst of these chapters, in which an objective arrangement is not possible, stands Peter's confession together with the first prediction of the Passion. The direct announcement of it is introduced at this point, after it has been shown throughout the Gospel up to this point that the authority of Christ is not manifest in splendor and in might. Thus his home town rejects him (13:53-58); John is put to death, and Jesus can do nothing to alter the situation (14:1-12). Those who remain true to him are able to do so only as they confess their faith in him (16:23-33). Between the two predictions of the Passion is the account of the Transfiguration. As at his baptism Jesus is now endorsed by his Father in view of the path of suffering that lies before him.

The other groupings of Jesus' words and deeds have all been encountered before. As to miracles and healings, ch. 15:21-28 should be singled out. Here Jesus acknowledges the great faith of the Canaanite woman and heals her daughter, although saying on his own behalf: "I was sent only to the lost sheep of the house of Israel." The effect of Jesus' activity forces its way already beyond his own nation, the ancient people of God. Ch. 17:14-19 also contains something new: Jesus heals an epileptic boy whom his disciples are unable to heal. Even though Jesus had given them authority to heal, they are not like the Master himself.

In the disputes with the Pharisees, ch. 15:10-20 indicates how Jesus nullified the ritual prescriptions concerning purity and overstepped likewise the borders of the people of God's ancient covenant.

The beginnings of a new partnership with a new order emerges despite the expectation of an end that is near (16:27 f.). At this point the question is raised whether the disciples should pay the temple tax any longer (17:24-27). The dispute among the disciples as to rank is utterly repudiated by Jesus (18:1-5). Ch. 18:15-20 indicates what steps should be taken when an offense occurs in the church. In this connection the power of binding and loosing (18:18) is given to Jesus' church, also the honor that grants her the presence of her Lord (18:20).

C. THE ROAD TO JERUSALEM (Matt. 19—20)

1. Concerning marriage and divorce (19:1-2)
2. Jesus blesses the children (19:13-15)
3. The rich young man and observations on wealth (19:16-26)
4. Peter's question concerning reward (19:27-30)
5. The parable of the workers in the vineyard (20:1-16)
6. The third prediction of the Passion (20:17-19)
7. The request of the mother of James and John (20:20-28)
8. Two blind men on the road to Jericho (20:29-34)

Ch. 19 begins with the note that Jesus went from Galilee to Judea. (In the case of all three Gospels the three following pericopes occur at this point.) The third announcement of the Passion belongs to this departure toward Judea (20:17-19). "Behold, we are going up to Jerusalem . . . , " Jesus says. The other pericopes have no essential relationship with it nor with one another. Three times in these stories the question of reward is dealt with: in the parable of the workers in the vineyard, in the question of Peter, and in the petition of the mother of the two disciples. Jesus does not flatly reject the question concerning reward but gives it a new direction. "You do not know what you are asking," he declares. "Are you able to drink the cup that I am to drink?"— Even along the path to suffering Jesus continues to be the Savior (20:29-34).

D. IN JERUSALEM (Matt. 21—25)

1. The entrance into Jerusalem (21:1-11)
2. The driving out of the money-changers from the temple (21:12-17)
3. The fig tree (21:18-22)
4. The question concerning Jesus' authority (21:23-27)
5. The parable of the two sons (21:28-32)
6. The parable of the wicked tenants of the vineyard (21:33-46)
7. The parable of the royal wedding feast (22:1-14)
8. The question of the Pharisees (the tribute money) (22:15-22)
9. The question of the Sadducees (the resurrection) (22:23-33)
10. The question as to the greatest commandment (22:34-40)
11. Jesus' question to the Pharisees concerning the Messiah (22:41-46)
12. The warning against the Pharisees (23:1-12)
13. Woes pronounced on the scribes (23:13-36)
14. Lament over Jerusalem (23:37-39)

Chapters 21—23, beginning with the entrance into Jerusalem, have as their essential feature the discussion of Jesus with the authorities in the Jewish community. In his symbolic act of entering into Jerusalem he asserted his claim to be the promised king of

Israel, marching into his city (Zech. 9:9), but a king veiled in humility. He demonstrates his claim by driving out the money-changers from the temple. His opponents then question him concerning his authority, and he reprimands them for the question by a counter-question. There follow a number of other questions, by which his opponents seek to entrap him, and Jesus again asks other questions, which silence them.

Following this controversial discussion is a warning that Jesus directs against the behavior of the Pharisees. This is coupled with an admonition to his disciples to show forth humility: "You have one teacher and you are all brethren" (23:8).

The long address of woes against the Pharisees conforms perfectly with the prophetic words of judgment in the Old Testament. The prophetic vehemence there also turned against a piety that had become hollow.

In between are three parables (21:28—22:14), all three of which are a part of this controversy from different aspects. This large complex section in Matthew demonstrates most clearly that in Jesus there is to be found not only the message of salvation but also the denunciatory message of the prophets of Israel. The section terminates in a lament over Jerusalem (23:37-39), which is quite close in character to Jeremiah's laments over this city before its first destruction.

E. THE COMING OF THE END (The Synoptic Apocalypse)
(Matt. 24—25)

1. Announcement of Jerusalem's destruction (24:1-2)
2. The beginning of the woes (24:3-14)
3. The horrors of the final age (24:15-28)
4. The coming of the Son of man (24:29-31)
5. The exact moment no one knows (24:32-36)
6. An admonition to vigilance (24:37-44)
7. The faithful and the indolent servant (24:45-51)
8. Parable of the ten virgins (25:1-13)
9. Parable of the talents held in trust (25:14-30)
10. Parable of the final judgment (25:31-46)

Just as indictments and announcements of judgment belong together in the prophets, so in Matthew the denunciation of the Pharisees and Sadducees is followed here by the announcement of final judgment. In order to read this part of the Gospel perceptively it is important to realize that there is here a later compilation of individual utterances (even as in the case of the Sermon on the Mount). The words have been uttered at various times and in different situations; and they would be misunderstood if one chose to fashion from them a coherent picture of the final age.

The theme that links together the apocalyptic descriptions in ch. 25 and the parables in ch. 25 is the summons to vigilance. The emphasis does not lie on fixing the stages of the final event, but stress is laid rather on the surprising effect of the bursting in of the final age and the return of Christ (24:27). (It is compared to lightning, vv. 32 ff. No one knows the exact hour.) Prior to this the gospel of the kingdom will be preached throughout the whole world (24:14). This word will indeed go beyond the immediate expectation of the end (24:34). The words of promise, however, will outlast all the catastrophes of the final age: "Heaven and earth will pass away, but my words will not pass away" (24:35).

F. SUFFERING, DEATH, AND RESURRECTION
(Matt. 26—28)

1. From the plot of death to Gethsemane (26:1-46)

    a.   The plot of death (26:1-5)

    b.   The anointing at Bethany (25:6-13)

    c.   Judas' betrayal (26:14-16, 20-25)

    d.   The Last Supper (26:17-19, 26-29)

    e.   Gethsemane (26:30-46)

In the Passion story there is little need to provide biblical information, because here we have a continuous account, and one gains a clear impression of the events in their sequence, as one reads and listens to these chapters in context. The decision of his enemies to kill him and of a disciple to betray him forms a framework around the account of how one of those for whom Jesus suffered paid him homage.

At the beginning of his pathway to death Jesus links the public worship of the old covenant with that of the new by instituting the Lord's Supper. In his suffering the history of sacrifice reaches its fulfillment.

2. From the arrest of Jesus to his death (26:47—27:66)

    a. The arrest (26:47-56)
    b. Before the Sanhedrin (26:57-68)
    c. Peter's betrayal (26:69-75)
    d. The end of Judas (27:3-10)
    e. Jesus before Pontius Pilate (27:1-2, 11-26)
    f. The mocking of Jesus (27:27-31)
    g. His crucifixion and death (27:32-56)
    h. His burial and the guard at the tomb (27:57-66)

The Jewish authorities in the spiritual realm and the Roman magistrates in the secular realm joined in convicting Jesus and in putting him to death. But the real impulse issued from the Jewish religious community, which saw their worship and faith threatened by Jesus. In his suffering and death, however, Jesus was no longer their opponent, as previously in the controversial discourses, but he accepted his suffering and bore it silently as the Servant of the Lord, who suffered also for his opponents (Isa. 53). In his cry of despair from the cross (27:46=Ps. 22:1) he involved himself in the lament of those who suffered among the ancient people of God, and he brought this lament to its conclusion.

3. The empty tomb and the resurrection

    a. The empty tomb (28:1-10)
    b. The guards at the tomb (28:11-15)
    c. Jesus' appearance before the disciples and his missionary command (28:16-20)

III

The Gospel of Mark

The "Book of the Secret Epiphanies," a title which Dibelius* has given to this Gospel, is characterized by the battle that is waged against the Satanic powers when Jesus comes with divine power. Nevertheless, this Gospel places the greatest emphasis on the obscure character of the messianic glory, the theme of the "messianic secret." †

The structure of the Gospel is simple; its language, very terse; and it moves on the whole at a much more rapid pace from Jesus' first appearance to his Passion, because the more extensive speech sections have been omitted.

It is in Mark that the saving message concerning Jesus' coming, suffering, and resurrection gets the name "gospel." The book is thus more a word with contemporary significance than an account concerning the past.

A. JESUS IN GALILEE (Mark 1—9)

1. The beginning of Jesus' public appearance (1:1-45)

    a. John the Baptist. Jesus' baptism and temptation (1:1-13)
    b. The message of Jesus (1:14-15)
    c. The calling of the first disciples (1:16-20)
    d. Stories of healing (1:21-45)

---

*Martin Dibelius, *From Tradition to Gospel* (New York: Scribner, 1935), p. 230.

†William Wrede, *Das Messiasgeheimnis in den Evangelien.* Göttingen: Vandenhoeck and Ruprecht, 1901.

(1) The healing in Capernaum of one possessed by a demon (1:21-28)
(2) Peter's mother-in-law and many sick (1:29-39)
(3) The healing of a leper (1:40-45)

Mark includes nothing whatsoever of Jesus' early life and reports but briefly on John the Baptist, Jesus' baptism and temptation. The message of Jesus is summarized at the beginning in one sentence: "The time is fulfilled, and the kingdom of God is at hand; repent, and believe in the gospel" (1:18, cf. also v. 22).

In the call of Simon and Andrew one comes across the term "immediately" * for the first time, an expression that is so characteristic of Mark's narrative.

From the very beginning Jesus' action stands side by side with his word. Thus in the three stories of healing, God's power to heal enters into the need of those who are suffering, and the spectators note with astonishment, "He commands even the unclean spirits and they obey him" (1:27). Jesus forbids the leper whom he has healed to tell about his cleansing (vv. 40-45); nevertheless, "people come to him from every quarter" (v. 45).

2. Controversial talks (2:1—3:6)

a. The healing of the paralytic (an offense caused by Jesus' forgiving sins) (2:1-12)
b. The calling of Levi (an offense caused by Jesus' association with sinners) (2:13-17)
c. The failure of Jesus' disciples to fast (2:18-22)
d. Gleaning on the Sabbath (2:23-28)
e. Healing on the Sabbath (the withered hand) (3:1-6)
f. "How can Satan cast out Satan?" (3:22-30)

*   *   *   *   *

Additional stories related to those of ch. 1:
(1) The healing of many sick people by the sea (3:7-12)
(2) The calling of the twelve disciples (3:13-19)
(3) The true kinsmen of Jesus (3:20-21, 31-35)

---

*Translator's Note: The term (Greek *euthus*) occurs 42 times in Mark. Luke uses it only once.

In his healing activity Jesus clashed with the Pharisees. All the important examples of the way he offended them have been brought together here. Thus the Pharisees were offended because he granted forgiveness (2:1-12) and ate together with tax collectors and sinners (2:13-17), because his disciples did not strictly observe the laws of fasting and of the Sabbath (2:18-28). They took offense because Jesus performed acts of healing on the Sabbath (3:1-6). Already here at the end of this section the leaders decide on his destruction (3:6). Jesus' reply to the charge that he was driving out demons by Beelzebub (3:22-30) also belongs in the section containing his disputes with the Jewish leaders.

In addition to the healings of the sick in ch. 1 there is included here a summary concerning the healing of many who were ill (3:7-12). The unclean spirits recognized him as the Son of God, but Jesus commanded them not to reveal it.

The calling of the twelve apostles (3:13-19) is an addition to ch. 1:16-20. They were his true kinsmen rather than his natural brothers who desired to curb his activity (3:20 f., 31-35).

3. Three Parables (4:1-20, 26-34)

    a. The sower (4:1-9). The interpretation (4:14-20)
    b. The significance of the parabolic address (4:10-13)
    c. The seed growing by itself (4:26-29)
    d. The mustard seed (4:30-34)

All three parables, from different points of view, are concerned with the quiet, apparently futile effect of Jesus' message. The parable of the seed, growing by itself, is peculiar to Mark. It is an unusually clear example of the parabolic type of utterance, which is able to comment on the coming of God's kingdom in the imagery of simple, everyday events. Insofar as only a few people (only the believers) understood them, they were also an expression of the messianic secret (vv. 10-13).

4. The light under a bushel (4:21-25)

5. Miracle stories (4:35—5:43)

    a. The stilling of the storm (4:35-41)

    b. The healing of the Gerasene demoniac (5:1-20)

    c. The healing of the woman with a flow of blood and the raising of the daughter of Jairus (5:21-43)

All these stories, told in such striking detail, have in common the feature that Jesus was a man among men, a mighty Lord, who in many ways proved himself to be such a Master. This explains why the reality of evil spirits is represented in detail. Driven out of the sick man, they had to find another dwelling place, and enter into a herd of swine. It explains why Jesus was conscious of power having left him when the sick woman, imploring his help, touched him. It explains the awed question of those who witnessed Jesus' stilling the storm: "Who then is this, that even wind and sea obey him?" (4:41).

6. From the rejection in Nazareth to the predictions of the Passion (6:1—9:32)

    a. Miscellaneous events:

        (1) The rejection in Nazareth (6:1-6)

        (2) The commissioning of the twelve (6:7-13)

        (3) The execution of John the Baptist (6:14-29)

        (4) Peter's confession and the first announcement of the Passion (8:27-33)

        (5) The Transfiguration (9:2-13)

        (6) The second announcement of the Passion (9:30-32)

The events that characterize the pathway of Jesus are the same in this section as in the Gospel of Matthew. The execution of John the Baptist, however, is told in much greater detail. Ch. 6:7-13 corresponds to the address in Matt. 10 at the time Jesus commissioned the disciples.

    b. Miracle stories in Mark 6—9:

        (1) The feeding of the 5,000 (6:30-44), the 4,000 (8:1-10)

        (2) Walking on the sea (6:45-52)

        (3) The healing of many sick people (6:53-56)

        (4) The Canaanite mother (7:24-30)

(5) The deaf-mute ("Ephphatha!")* (7:31-37)
(6) The blind man in Bethsaida (8:22-26)
(7) The epileptic boy (the failure of the disciples) (9:14-29)

Also in these stories of healing Mark emphasizes the effects of the power that issued from Jesus. They are portrayed here often more concretely and in greater detail than in the other Gospels. The power of healing, however, had to be matched by faith. This was especially evident in the case of the Canaanite mother and the father of the epileptic boy, who made the comment: "I believe, Lord, help my unbelief!" (9:24).

   c. The controversial talks in Mark 6—9:
       (1) The greater commandment (7:1-13)
       (2) The things that defile a man (7:14-23)
       (3) The Pharisees demand a sign (8:11-13)
       (4) A warning against the leaven of the Pharisees (8:14-21)

Mark contrasts the external regulations of the Pharisees and the rite of handwashing with the Fourth Commandment in greater detail than does Matthew. He represents Jesus as saying: "You thus make void the word of God through your tradition" (7:13).

   d. The instruction of the disciples in Mark 6—9:
       (1) Concerning discipleship (8:34—9:1)
       (2) The dispute about status (9:33-37)
       (3) The unknown exorcist (9:38-41)
       (4) Temptation (9:42-50)

Ch. 9:38-41 is peculiar to Mark. In contrast to the disciples, Jesus accepted exorcism of demons in his name, even when it was done by one who did not follow him. He declared: "For he that is not against us is for us" (9:40). Even a cup of water given to the disciples, because they belong to Christ, is a deed done for Christ.

Much in 9:42-50 is obscure, furnishing a little hint of how limited our knowledge of Jesus and his disciples is.

---

*Translator's Note: The term "Ephphatha" used here by Jesus in addressing the deaf-mute is an Aramaic expression, meaning "Be opened!"

B. THE ROAD TO JERUSALEM (Mark 10:1-52)

1. Concerning marriage and divorce (10:1-12)
2. Blessing of the children (10:13-16)
3. The rich young man. Concerning riches (10:17-27)
4. Peter's question regarding reward (10:28-31)
5. The third announcement concerning the Passion (10:32-34)
6. The question of James and John (10:35-45)
7. The healing of blind Bartimaeus (10:46-52)

In this section there are two important utterances of Jesus about himself. They can be properly understood only when taken together. To the rich young man Jesus said: "Why do you call me good? No one is good except God alone" (10:18). And to the disciples, who were concerned about securing a privileged position, he said: "The Son of man also came not to be served but to serve and to give his life as a ransom for many" (10:45).

C. IN JERUSALEM (Mark 11—13)

1. The entrance into Jerusalem (11:1-11)
2. The driving out of the money-changers from the temple (11:15-19)
3. The barren fig tree (11:12-14, 20-25)
4. The rebuke of the question concerning authority (11:27-33)
5. The parable of the wicked tenants of the vineyard (12:1-12)
6. The question of the Pharisees (concerning the tribute money) (12:13-17)
7. The question of the Sadducees (concerning the resurrection) (12:18-27)
8. The question concerning the greatest commandment (12:28-34)
9. Jesus' question to the Pharisees concerning the Messiah (12:35-37)
10. The warning against the scribes (12:38-40)
11. The widow's mite (12:41-44)
12. The coming of the end (13:1-37)
    a. The announcement of the destruction of the temple (13:1-2)
    b. The beginning of the travail (13:3-13)
    c. The terrors of the end of time (13:14-23)
    d. The return of the Son of man (13:24-27)
    e. "That hour no one knows!" (13:28-32)
    f. An admonition to vigilance (13:33-37)

Mark emphasizes the last section (which begins here) by repeating from 3:6 the decision of the leaders to destroy Jesus. Otherwise Mark in this section agrees for the most part with Matthew, except for passages that Matthew has in addition to Mark. The difference in ch. 12:28-34, however, is significant. Thus in Matthew and Luke the question concerning the greatest commandment is asked for the purpose of tempting Jesus (Matt. 22:35; Luke 10:25). In Mark, however, it is intended to be a legitimate question. The scribe agrees with Jesus' answer, and, Jesus says to him: "You are not far from the kingdom of God!" This agreement with the scribe is significant because Jesus' reply consists simply of two citations from the Old Testament: the acknowledgment of the one God in Deut. 6:4 (a statement uttered in every Jewish worship service) and the commandment concerning love in Lev. 19:18 from the Holiness Code.* In this Mark thus saw the church of Jesus to be in full agreement with the faith of the Old Testament.

The discourse about the coming of the final age is shorter in Mark than in Matthew and Luke. The admonition to be vigilant, however, is especially emphasized in his conclusion (13:33-37). Special attention is called to the position of doorkeeper in the parable of the master away on a journey: "And what I say to you I will say to all: Watch!" (13:37).

D. JESUS' SUFFERING, DEATH, AND RESURRECTION
(Mark 14—16)

1. From the plot against Jesus' life to Gethsemane (Mark 14)

    a. The plot against Jesus' life (14:1-2)
    b. The anointing in Bethany (14:3-9)
    c. Judas' betrayal (14:10-11, 17-21)
    d. The Last Supper (14:12-16, 22-25)
    e. Gethsemane (14:26-42)

2. From Jesus' arrest to his death (14:43—15:47)

    a. The arrest (14:43-52)

---

*Translator's Note: Cf. Westermann, *Handbook to the Old Testament* (Minneapolis: Augsburg, 1967), pp. 68-70.

    b. Before the Sanhedrin (14:53-65)
    c. Peter's denial (14:66-72)
    d. Jesus before Pontius Pilate (15:1-15)
    e. The mockery of Jesus (15:16-20)
    f. Jesus' crucifixion and death (15:21-41)
    g. Jesus' burial (15:42-47)

3. The empty tomb and the resurrection (16)

    a. The empty tomb (16:1-8)
    b. Appearance of the Risen One. The commissioning of the disciples, and the exaltation of Jesus to the right hand of God (a later addition) (16:9-20)

Although this entire closing portion agrees essentially with Matthew, the narrative of the empty tomb with which Mark closes sounds strikingly different from that in Matthew, as may be noted in comparing the two:

Matthew 28:8	Mark 16:8
"So they departed from the tomb with fear and great joy, and ran to tell his disciples."	"And they went out and fled from the tomb; for trembling and astonishment had come upon them. And they said nothing to anyone, for they were afraid."

The later supplement (vv. 9-20) is missing in the oldest manuscripts. It was added about the middle of the second century. The section is a kind of harmony of the Gospels, summing up the resurrection account in all the Gospels. There are, in addition, some supplements.

Verses 9-11 correspond to John 20:11-18; vv. 12-13 to Luke 24:13-35; vv. 14-16 to Matthew 28:16-20; v. 19 to Luke 24:50-53. Verse 20 even contemplates the activity of Jesus' messengers in all the world:

> "And they went forth and preached everywhere, while the Lord worked with them and confirmed the message by the signs that attended it."

IV

The Gospel of Luke

Luke is the Gospel that has the most pronounced historical concerns of the three Synoptic Gospels. It is part of a historical work that is continued in the Acts of the Apostles, originating with the same author.

Luke perceives history as a whole, divided into three successive epochs: the age of Israel, the time of Jesus on earth, and the period from Jesus' ascension until his coming again. From this point of view Jesus is conceived to be "the center of history *(Zeit)*" [*] The second epoch is presented by the Gospel; the third epoch by the Acts of the Apostles. The first epoch is related intimately with the Gospel by its allusions to the fulfillment of Old Testament prophecy. This is evident especially in the early account of Jesus' childhood (chs. 1–2).

Because of this historical view rooted in *Heilsgeschichte* the expectation of Jesus' immediately imminent return recedes into the background. A comment like that in Mark 1:15, "The time is fulfilled, and the kingdom of God is at hand," is not found in Luke. Instead, the Gospel attempts more forcefully than the other Gospels to present Jesus' activity in an unbroken continuity, even as the Prologue states in 1:1-4: "It seemed good to me also, having followed all things closely for some time past, to write an orderly account . . . . " It sets the events concerning Jesus of Nazareth more than once within the context of world history (2:1; 3:1). Thus Jesus' activity is arranged more definitely into periods in Luke. The early childhood (chs. 1–2), which is worked out in such detail only in Luke, is followed by the account of Jesus' activity in Galilee (chs. 3–9). Then in definite contrast to this comes the so-called "Lukan Travel Account" (9:51–18:14), telling of Jesus'

---

[*]Hans Conzelmann, *The Theology of St. Luke* (New York: Harper & Bros., 1960), pp. 170-206.

progress toward the Passion, his activity in Jerusalem (chs. 19–21), and finally the actual Passion story itself (chs. 22–24).

As sources in addition to Mark, whose plan he extensively follows, Luke makes use of the so-called Q source (as does also Matthew) and also much material of his own. In passages peculiar to Luke there is a feature that stands out prominently: Jesus is the Savior of sinners. His work is concerned especially with the poor and lowly. At the same time, Luke calls special attention to the messiahship of Jesus, announced in the Old Testament. But more clearly than in Matthew and Mark emerges the account of how Christ's work extends to the Gentiles (e.g., 2:10; 4:24-27).

A. THE EARLY LIFE OF JESUS (Luke 1—2)

1. The foreword to Theophilus (1:1-4) S *

2. The birth announcements (1:5-56) S

    a. The announcements of John's birth (1:5-25)

    b. The announcement of Jesus' birth (1:26-38)

    c. Mary's visit to Elizabeth (1:39-56)
        "The *Magnificat*" (vv. 46-55)

3. The birth accounts (1:57—2:40) S

    a. The birth of John (1:57-66, 80)
        "The *Benedictus*" (vv. 67-79)

    b. The birth of Jesus (2:1-20)
        "The *Gloria in excelsis*" (v. 14)

    c. Jesus' circumcision and presentation in the temple (2:21-40)
        "The *Nunc Dimittis*" (vv. 29-32)

4. The twelve-year-old boy in the temple (2:41-52) S

The account of Jesus' early life within the Gospel as a whole has the function of linking the new epoch with the old covenant;

---

*Translator's Note: The letter "S" indicates source material peculiar to Luke. When this material is mixed with Markan material the "S" will be enclosed in brackets. Cf. below pp. 43, 45, 46.

the era beginning with Christ's coming, with that which preceded it.

In language closely resembling that of the Old Testament, it tells how the message spread abroad in the way God's people of the old covenant awaited it. They were represented by the fathers and mothers, priests and prophets—above all, however, by the poor (the shepherds), who received the promise: "He whom you await is come!"

The events that are reported have the significance of signs, confirming the joyful message. (Compare the word of the angel: "And this shall be a sign for you"—2:12.) The motif concerning message, so important to the Old Testament, is adopted here and brought to its climax. Along with this, as a second primary theme in this story of Jesus' early life, is the way the Old Testament praise of God becomes the jubilant, God-extolling response of those who accept the message.*

This early history of the life of Christ is thus interspersed with songs that resemble precisely the Psalms. In their midst is the *Gloria in excelsis,* which the angels begin singing, as they appropriate the hymn of the seraphim from Isa. 6. The announcement concerning John and Jesus, as well as the account of their birth, is narrated in parallel fashion. The response of praise for both is also similar. As children of God's ancient covenant people, Jesus and John belong together. They stand at the end of the line of prophets and effect its fulfillment. The intimate relationship between the Old and New Testaments receives its most lovely expression in this early history.

B. THE ACTIVITY OF JESUS IN GALILEE†
(Luke 3:1—9:50)‡

1. John the Baptist and Jesus' baptism (3:1-22)

    a. The Baptist's appearance and his sermon on repentance (3:1-9)
    b. The Baptist's sermon concerning the social ranks (3:10-14) S
    c. The allusion to Jesus as the Messiah (3:15-18)

---

*Translator's Note: Cf. C. Westermann, *op. cit.,* pp. 60, 109, 221.
†Translator's Note: See maps of Jesus' ministry (inside front cover).
‡Compare the survey of p. 14 f.

d. The arrest of the Baptist (3:19-20) S
e. Jesus' baptism (3:21-22)

2. Jesus' genealogy (3:23-38)

The real account of Jesus of Nazareth begins at this point. Luke accordingly places this beginning in a historical sequence by indicating in 3:1 the year of Caesar's reign and the name of the governor of Judea.* He includes also the old prophetic introductory phrase: "The word of God came to . . . " (3:2).

Peculiar to Luke is the Baptist's sermon to the professional groups (3:10-14). He responds to those who come to him from different ranks, asking: "What shall we do?" stirred as they have been by his sermon on repentance.

Luke's genealogy differs from that of Matthew in that it extends Jesus' lineage from Joseph back to Adam. The genealogy of Matthew starts with Abraham. Both, however, represent the ancestral line of Joseph, not that of Mary.

3. The temptation of Jesus and the beginning of his public appearance (4:1-30)

a. His temptation (4:1-13)
b. His appearance in Galilee (4:14-15)
c. His inaugural sermon in Nazareth (4:16-30) S

Luke's introduction to the activity of Jesus in Galilee is in 4:16-30. Jesus interpreted a portion of Scripture in the synagogue of his home town, quite in accordance with the custom of the worship service. The feature that was new in this was the way he applied Isa. 61:1-2 to himself. The passage was understood in his time as a prophecy of the Messiah. Jesus declared: "Today this scripture is fulfilled in your hearing!" (4:21). The claim that he asserted in this announcement aroused indignation, and the story then becomes an account concerning the way he was rejected in Nazareth, mentioned also by the other Gospels (Matt. 13:53-58; Mark 6:1-6). In a different way from these Gospels, however, Jesus cites two

---

*Translator's Note: Also the name of other rulers: Herod, tetrarch of Galilee; Philip, tetrarch of Ituraea and Trachonitis; and Lysanius, tetrarch of Abilene, including also the high priests Annas and Caiaphas.

scriptural examples concerning the way Elijah and Elisha had directly helped the Gentiles (1 Kings 17; 2 Kings 5). The angry listeners then thrust him out of the city in order to cast him head-long from the brow of the hill. "But passing through the midst of them he went away" (4:30). Here already in the introduction are all the decisive motifs: Jesus is the Redeemer, promised in the Old Testament. This claim of his, however, results in his being rejected by his own people. There is an intimation of the way in which the gospel will be passed on to the Gentiles. There is also already a resolve to kill Jesus and the failure of this plan.

4. The miracles of healing (4:31–5:26; 6:17-19)

   a. The man possessed with a demon in the synagogue at Capernaum (4:31-37)
   b. The healing of Peter's mother-in-law and others (4:38-44)
   c. Peter's catch of fish (5:1-11) S
   d. The leper (5:12-16)
   e. The lame man (forgiveness of sins) (5:17-26)
   f. The healing of many who were sick (6:17-19)

5. The hostility of the Pharisees (5:17–6:16)

   a. [The lame man (the forgiveness of sins) (5:17-26)]
   b. The calling of Levi (5:27-32)
   c. The question concerning fasting (5:33-39)
   d. The disciples' gleaning of grain on the Sabbath (6:1-5)
   e. Healing on the Sabbath (6:6-11)
   f. The calling of the twelve disciples (6:12-16)

Both these groups of passages agree essentially with Matthew and Mark or with one of them. The story of the healing in 5:17-26 links the two groups of passages together. At this point the scribes and Pharisees come forward and begin to assail Jesus in his saving activity.

Three accounts concerning the calling of the disciples have been combined with the two above-mentioned groups of passages that are otherwise essentially unified. Thus the nucleus of his church, the first band of disciples, arose at the same time as he performed healing and responded to charges leveled against him.

Peculiar to Luke is the story of Peter's great catch of fish. In the miracle that Jesus performs for him, Simon, the fisherman, is confronted by the living reality of God and becomes terrified (cf. Isa. 6). Along with the exhortation: "Do not be afraid!" is issued the call to discipleship, which he, together with certain comrades, immediately obeys.

6. The Sermon on the Plain (6:20-49)

    a. "Blessed!—Woe" (6:20-26) S
    b. Be merciful! (6:27-38)
    c. The speck and the log (6:39-42)
    d. Good and evil fruit (6:43-46)
    e. The two houses (6:47-49)

Luke's "Sermon on the Plain" corresponds to the Sermon on the Mount in Matthew. It contains, however, far fewer utterances.* It lacks, above all, the antithetical statements that give to the Sermon on the Mount its distinctive character. ("You have heard . . . but I say to you" Matt. 5:21-28.) The Beatitudes in Luke differ from those in Matthew in that they are matched by cries of "Woe!" (6:24-26). The first Beatitudes are also plainly assigned to the poor and hungry. (In Matthew they were addressed to the poor in spirit and to those who hunger and thirst after righteousness.) In the part that follows, Luke emphasizes the commandment of love toward one's enemies. Otherwise there are no essential differences from the corresponding words in the Sermon on the Mount.

7. Miscellaneous material (7:1—9:50)

    a. The centurion in Capernaum (7:1-10)
    b. The young man at Nain (7:11-17) S
    c. The Baptist's question and Jesus' reply (7:18-35)
    d. The anointing of Jesus by the sinful woman (7:36-50) S
    e. The ministering women (8:1-3) S
    f. The parable of the sower and its significance (8:4-18)
    g. The true relatives (8:19-21)
    h. Stilling the storm (8:22-25)
    i. The healing of the demoniac (the swineherd) (8:26-39)
    j. The woman with the flow of blood and the daughter of Jairus (8:40-56)

---

*Some sayings occur later.

k. Commissioning the twelve disciples (9:1-6, 10)
l. Herod is perplexed concerning Jesus (9:7-9)
m. Feeding the five thousand (9:11-17)
n. Peter's confession and the first announcement of the Passion (9:18-22)
o. Utterances concerning discipleship (9:23-27)
p. The Transfiguration (9:28-36)
q. The healing of the epileptic boy (9:37-43a)
r. The second announcement of the Passion (9:43b-45)
s. The quarrel over status among the disciples (9:46-48)
t. The unknown exorcist (9:49-50)

Chapters 7 and 8 begin and end with the accounts of healing. Material peculiar to Luke is the story of the raising of the young man at Nain. It is characteristic of Luke in that it deals with Jesus' compassion for the poor and miserable. To the poor widow he restores her only son (7:15).

Following the question of John the Baptist and Jesus' response concerning his messiahship, there are two passages (unique to Luke) that continue this reply. The one is the account of Jesus' anointing by the sinful woman. Included is his parable of the two creditors (7:40-43). This is along the line often stressed by Luke, in which Jesus is presented as the Savior of sinners. The other passage is the note concerning the women who followed him and provided for him* out of their means (8:1-3).

The remaining passages in chapter 8 correspond to those in Matthew and Mark. Everything in 9:1-50 matches Matthew and Mark in order and essential content.

C. THE LUKAN TRAVEL ACCOUNT (Luke 9:51—18:14)
1.

a. Turning toward Jerusalem. The Samaritan village (9:51-56) S
b. Three different would-be followers of Jesus (9:57-62)
c. Commissioning the seventy disciples (10:1-12)
d. Woes pronounced upon Chorazin, Bethsaida, and Capernaum (10:13-16)
e. The return of the seventy disciples (10:17-24) S

---

*Translator's Note: The author has adopted the reading "him" (Greek *autó*) in 8:3 attested by some ancient authorities, in place of "them" (Greek *autois*) which R.S.V. follows. Compare R.S.V. margin.

All these passages are concerned directly or indirectly with the disciples and discipleship. Material peculiar to Luke consists of 9:51-56, 61-62; 10:17-20. A new division begins in 9:51 ff. with the account of Jesus' turning from now on toward Jerusalem. Everything that then follows is on the way that brings him to the place of his death. The incident concerning the Samaritan village indicates already that those who failed to accept him were also included in his mercy. This is something, however, that the disciples did not yet comprehend. Nevertheless, judgment threatens those who despise the words and activity of the Savior (10:13-16). The same high position is accorded also the activity of the disciples (10:10-12, 17-20).

2.

a. The question concerning the supreme commandment (10:25-28)
b. The good Samaritan (10:29-37) S
c. Mary and Martha (10:38-42)
d. Concerning prayer (11:1-13) [S]
   The importunate friend (vv. 5-8)
e. The evil spirits (11:14-26)
f. The blessed mother of Jesus (11:27-28) S
g. The sign of Jonah (11:29-32)
h. The light under the bushel (11:33-36)

It is only in Luke that the parable of the good Samaritan occurs, following the question about the supreme commandment. Unique also is the illustration concerning Mary and Martha. In similar vein is the response of Jesus to the woman who pronounced a blessing on his mother, "Blessed are those who hear the word of God and keep it!" (11:27 ff., found only in Luke).

3.

a. The discourse against the Pharisees (11:37—12:1)
b. The admonition to acknowledge Jesus (12:2-12)
c. The rich farmer (12:13-21) S
d. Anxiety and the gathering of treasure (12:22-34)
e. Vigilance and fidelity (12:35-48)
f. The seriousness of the coming time (12:49-53) [S]

    g. The signs of the time (12:54-56)
    h. An admonition to become reconciled (12:57-59)

The parable of the rich farmer is a warning against a security which death shatters. The whole section points to the seriousness of the age that was lying before the disciples. "I came to send a fire on the earth and would that it were already kindled," Jesus says (12:49 ff.).

4.

    a. The tower of Siloam (13:1-5)
    b. The barren fig tree (13:6-9) S
    c. The healing of the crippled woman (13:10-17) S
    d. The mustard and the leaven (13:18-21)
    e. The narrow gate (13:22-30)
    f. Today, tomorrow, and on the third day (13:31-33) S
    g. Pronouncement of judgment upon Jerusalem (13:34-35)

In 13:31-33 the introductory statement of the Lukan travel account is again picked up. Jesus must go on his way today and tomorrow and do his work in the land. But then the third day awaits him, and on that day his work will be completed—in Jerusalem. "For it cannot be that a prophet should perish away from Jerusalem," he says (v. 33). Matching this statement is the utterance concerning repentance in 13:1-5 and the announcement of judgment upon Jerusalem in 13:34-35.

5.

    a. Healing of the man who had dropsy (14:1-6) S
    b. The sayings concerning banquets (14:7-14) S
    c. The great supper (14:15-24)
    d. Discipleship by bearing the cross (14:25-27)
    e. Building a tower and waging a war. Salt (14:28-35) S
    f. The lost sheep, coin, and son (15:1-32) S
    g. The unjust steward (16:1-13) S
    h. The rich man and Lazarus (16:19-31)
       The Pharisees and the law (16:14-18) [S]

This section has as its distinctive feature the set of parables unique to Luke. The three parables in ch. 15 at the heart of the Lukan travel document express most clearly how Luke understood the gospel of Jesus Christ. But the other two parables are also characteristic of Luke, each in its own way.

6.

a. Temptation, forgiveness, and faith (17:1-6)
b. "We are unworthy servants" (17:7-10) S
c. The ten lepers (17:11-19) S
d. The kingdom of God and the day of the Son of man (17:20-37) [S]
e. The ungodly judge (18:1-8) S
f. The Pharisee and the Publican (18:9-14)

Except for the series of utterances in 17:1-6 and the great discourse concerning the day of the Son of man, this section contains only Lukan material, bringing Luke's travel account to a close. The narrative about the healing of the ten lepers, which ends with the sentence: "Your faith has saved you," and the two parables all have to do with a particular manner of faith, namely, the faith that praises God for having experienced salvation (17:11-19), the faith that does not give up its earnest entreaty (18:1-8), the faith that confesses sin (18:9-14).

D. THE ROAD TO JERUSALEM (Luke 18:15—19:27)

1. Jesus blessing the children (18:15-17)
2. The rich young ruler (18:18-30)
3. The third announcement of the Passion (18:31-34)
4. The blind man at Jericho (18:35-43)
5. Zacchaeus (19:1-10) S
6. The pounds held in trust (19:11-27)

In 18:15 ff. the correspondence of Luke with the other Gospels again begins. All the passages covered in 18:15-43 are like those in Matthew and Mark. Only Luke 19:1-10 is unique, and here again the narrative concerns the Savior of sinners.

E. JESUS IN JERUSALEM (Luke 19:28—21:38)

1. The entrance into Jerusalem (Luke 19:28-40)
2. Jesus weeps over Jerusalem (19:41-44) S

In this entire section about Jesus in Jerusalem the only passages that are specifically Luke's are the account of how Jesus wept over Jerusalem (19:34-44) and the admonition to vigilance and sobriety at the conclusion (21:34-36). Jesus' lament over the impending destruction of the "city of God" at the beginning of the Passion story links Christ's work once more with the history of God's people of the old covenant. This is not all. In his lament over the city Jesus mentions in advance that his approaching suffering will concern also this city that is to condemn him.

F. THE SUFFERING, DEATH, AND RESURRECTION OF JESUS (Luke 22—24)

In the Passion story the correspondence between the three Gospels is so extensive that individual features are exceedingly few in number. Besides the minor differences in the story of the Last Supper, Luke includes Jesus' strange comment to his disciples afterwards (22:35-38). It has never been fully explained. One meets here the statement concerning the "two swords." They have been interpreted in the history of the church as referring to temporal and spiritual power.

Peculiar to Luke is also the account of how Pilate sent Jesus to Herod (23:6-12), and how Pilate then declared that Herod also had found no basis for an indictment.

In connection with Jesus' progress toward death Luke adds the account of the lament by the women of Jerusalem. Jesus responds to this in a mood like that of 19:41-44, when he wept over Jerusalem.

The episode of the robbers on the cross (23:39-43), bearing witness again to the Savior of sinners, is only in Luke.

The individuality and forcefulness of the Lukan account stand out exquisitely in the account of the disciples at Emmaus. It is reminiscent of the Old Testament stories concerning the coming of a divine messenger in human form, unrecognized until his departure. In conclusion, Luke indicates again* the important features of the Christ event at the center of time, referring back to the history of the old covenant and pointing forward to the period of missionary activity and the church.

---

*Cf. chs. 1 and 2.

V

The Gospel of John

The Fourth Gospel is not concerned with the completeness of the tradition concerning Jesus of Nazareth* but rather with the full development of the confession concerning him as the Son of God and Lord (20:31). It is so formulated at the heart of the Prologue in a way that is applicable to the whole Gospel:

> "And the Word became flesh and dwelt among us,
>   full of grace and truth;
>   we have beheld his glory, glory as of the only Son
>   from the Father" (1:14).

The Gospel as a whole develops this sentence. But even the various divisions of the Gospel can already be perceived in the Prologue. The three primary divisions correspond to the segments of vv. 11 f.:

1. Chs. 3-6: "He came to his own home" (v. 11a)
2. Chs. 7-12: "His own people received him not" (v. 11b)
3. Chs. 13-17: "But to all who received him . . . " (v. 12a)

The first division (chs. 3—6) centers around the two concepts mentioned in 1:4, viz., light (= truth) † and life ‡; the second division, around the concept of crisis (separation and judgment): the controversies in chs. 7—12. These are anticipated in v. 5 of the Prologue. Those of whom v. 12 declares: "They received him,"

---

*Cf. Luke 1:1-4.
†Especially in chs. 3-4.
‡Especially in chs. 5-6.

are the ones who speak in v. 14 and v. 16. They confess that they
have accepted what the Lord gave them in his farewell addresses
(chs. 13–17).

It is not until the Passion story (chs. 18–20) that John begins
to agree substantially with the Synoptic Gospels. It thus demonstrates clearly that the more abstract exposition of his confession
must at this point become once more a simple account of what
happened.

At the same time, however, the Passion story in John is interwoven with all the other parts of the Gospel more effectively than
in the case of the other three. This has been achieved by the comment concerning "the hour" (or "time"), a term which in the decisive passages refers to the goal toward which Jesus is moving.
It gives the Gospel as a whole a forward movement toward this
goal. This is evident in ch. 2,* which is a kind of prelude intro-
ducing the entire section (chs. 2–17), in 7:1-13,† and in ch. 12,‡
and in the conclusion to the Farewell Discourses.§ This forward
movement is expressed most forcibly in the contrast between the
festive banquet of ch. 2 and that of ch. 13. The former is dominated by the phrase: "My hour has not yet come" (2:4); the latter,
by the phrase: "My hour *has* come."

The outline of the book is as follows:

A. Prologue (1:1-18)

B. Introduction: The witnesses (1:19-51)

C. "We saw his glory" (2:1—17:26)
   1. Prelude: Life and judgment (2:1-25)
   2. "He came to his own home" (3:1—6:71)
      a. In his word (truth) (3:1—4:54)
      b. In his miracles (life) (5:1—6:71)
   3. "His own people did not receive him" (7:1—12:50)
   4. "But as many as received him" (Farewell speeches)
      (13:1—17:26)

---

*Translator's Note: Cf. 2:4: "My hour has not yet come."
†Translator's Note: Cf. 7:6: "My time has not yet come."
‡Translator's Note: Cf. 12:23: "The hour has come."
§Translator's Note: Cf. 17:1: "The hour has come."

D. "The Word became flesh" (18:1—21:25)
1. Suffering and death (18:1—19:25)
2. Resurrection (20:1-30)
3. Supplement: Manifestation at the Sea of Tiberias (21:1-25)

This may be presented in chart form as follows:

| 1:1-18 | 1-2 | 3-6 | 7-12 | 13 | 14-16 | 17 | 18-21 |

A. THE PROLOGUE (John 1:1-18)

The prologue of John is a hymn, as may be immediately recognized when one reads it without the additions inserted by the evangelist, viz., the comment concerning John the Baptist (vv. 6-8, 15) plus the appended clauses (vv. 13, 17).

The hymn can be easily memorized, if one has a grasp of its distinctive arrangement, viz., the way in which the second concept of one line is usually picked up and continued in the new line. In this way, the peculiar powerful rhythm of the phrases comes about:

a. The *Logos* (Word) at the beginning with God (vv. 1-2)
b. Creation, life, and light, coming by means of the *Logos* (vv. 3-4)
c. The resulting contrast, viz., light-darkness (vv. 5, 9-10)
d. Out of this the drama concerning the *Heilsgeschichte* (vv. 11-12).

The second part of the hymn is the confession of those who have experienced the effects of this drama (1:14 ff.) and must testify to it. This occurs in the Gospel, opening with the Prologue.

B. THE WITNESSES (John 1:19-51)

1. The testimony of John the Baptist (1:19-34)

The difference between John's Gospel and the first three Gospels is very evident here. The only one who points to Jesus is John the

Baptist. His activity is presented entirely under the concept of witness. The narrative account begins with the question "Who are you?" addressed to John, and he answers: "Only one who prepares the way" (vv. 19-28). As Jesus then comes to him, his first comment is: "This is he!" With this everything is stated. "I have borne witness," says John, "that this is the Son of God" (vv. 29-34).

2. The chain of witnesses (1:35-51)

John also directs his disciples to Jesus (vv. 35-40). In this way the link is established between the witness, preceding Jesus, and the multiplicity of witnesses, following him. The first disciples fetch others (vv. 41-44). Jesus calls Nathanael, who moves from his doubt to a jubilant acceptance (vv. 45-51).

C. "WE SAW HIS GLORY" (John 2:1—17:26)

1. Prelude: Jesus brings life and judgment (2:1-25)

The stories of the wedding at Cana (found only in John's Gospel) and the cleansing of the temple are both put at the beginning of the main section, because they are intended to illustrate the two sides of Jesus' activity: (1) the life, joy, and fulfillment which he brings (2) yet precisely with these, judgment, i.e., the separation that must take place in relation to his word. In both stories Jesus remains a solitary figure. His hour has not yet come (2:4). He does not confide in those who believe in him (2:23-25).

2. "He came to his own home" (3:1—6:71)

a. In his word (truth) (3:1—4:54)
   (1) To Nicodemus (3:1-21)
   (2) To the Baptist (3:22-36)
   (3) To the woman of Samaria (4:1-30)
   (4) Sowing and reaping (the messengers) (4:31-42)

Here a further peculiarity of John becomes apparent. It has long dialogues. These become discourses, in which the partner in the dialogue then completely withdraws. Each of these speeches, moreover, develops fundamental concepts, in which Jesus reveals himself as the One who was sent from God.

It is in his word that Jesus comes to all men. Educated and eminent Nicodemus approaches him with questions. Jesus himself goes to a simple woman at the well (a Samaritan at that) and talks to her. The educated Nicodemus does not understand him any better than the lowly woman. Nevertheless, in and through these individuals Jesus' word is to continue to have effect.

The conversation with Nicodemus (3:1-21) has to do with rebirth, a rebirth leading to the acceptance of salvation, presented here along quite broad lines. It is based on the gift of the Son of God to the world (3:16).

The conversation with the woman of Samaria (4:5-29) is concerned chiefly with "living water." Then as the conversation continues, the One who brings life is shown to be also the Revealer of truth. The question concerning the correct worship of God is thereby also answered. (Jesus' comment concerning "worship in spirit and in truth" in vv. 19-26 summarizes the conversations of chs. 3 and 4.)

The witnesses, however, belong to the revelation of truth. Therefore the witness of John (4:22-36) and that of the disciples (4:31-42) are here once more resumed. Even the Samaritan woman, who to be sure has understood nothing though sensing Jesus to be the bearer of truth, shares in the witness; for she brings back others. She is able then to withdraw (4:41) as does John the Baptist (3:30). It is important to note that there was an encounter with Jesus. All had a share, however, in the harvest (vv. 31-38).

   b. In his miraculous deeds (life) (4:43—6:71)
     (1) The official at Capernaum (4:43-54)
     (2) The sick man at the pool of Bethesda (5:1-16)
     (3) The Father and the Son. Life and judgment (5:17-47)
     (4) The feeding of the five thousand. Jesus walks on the sea (6:1-26)
     (5) The bread of life (6:27-59)
     (6) The confession of Peter (6:60-71)

Another peculiarity of John is shown in the way one of the miracles found also in the Synoptic Gospels is told. A long discourse is then appended to it. This develops its significance for revelation. One should not in any case, however, cause the miracles to evaporate into mere symbolic treatments. For without the actual material event the discourses which follow the miracles would lose their basis. If Jesus were not the Savior, working in that which is physical, he would also fail to be the revealer of the Father's love.

At the beginning are two stories of healing, which have been grouped together as illustrations for many others. In the one story healing is granted to the believer (4:43-54); in the other, there is a healing on the Sabbath day. This caused the Jews to hate him (5:1-16). The discourse that follows at this point fits in closely with the healings. The sick believed in him and received from him life— restored life. Jesus said to the Jews, who were attacking him: "You refuse to come to me that you may have life" (5:40). Nevertheless his work was only that which he had received from his Father. The Old Testament, which his opponents were carefully examining, bore witness concerning him. His present activity was also a testimony to him. The Father had entrusted him with life and judgment. But the Jews were unable to believe in him; for in the final analysis they were concerned with their own honor and not with God's cause.

The miracle of feeding the multitude (6:1-15) reveals Jesus as the one able to produce abundance. For this reason the people desire to make him king. Attached to this story is the discourse concerning the bread of life (6:26-59). The Jews considered the manna that their fathers ate in the wilderness the highest possible type of miracle. Over against it Jesus asserted his higher claim: "I am the bread of life" (v. 35). The remainder of the discourse is but a development of this one statement.

The confession of Peter (6:66-71) concludes this entire section. It is occasioned by the way in which many of Jesus' disciples now abandon him, because they are offended at his extravagant claim (vv. 60-65). Jesus then asks the Twelve: "Will you also go away?" and Peter answers on their behalf: "Lord, to whom shall we go? You have the words of eternal life; and we have believed, and have come to know, that you are the Holy One of God." Thus it is conclusively stated that the life Jesus has come to bring is granted only to believers. There is no other faith but the confession of Jesus as the Christ. The essence of a confession is expressed in

6:60-71 in an unusually clear way. For a comparison there is Josh.
24, where all the characteristic features of a confession are the same.

3. "His own people received him not" (7:1—12:50)

    a. Prelude: "The hour has not yet come" (7:1-13)
    b. Jesus at the Feast of Tabernacles (7:14-52)
    c. Jesus and the adulteress (8:1-11)
    d. The light of the world—separation (8:12-59)
    e. The healing of the man born blind (9:1-41)
    f. The shepherd (10:1-42)
    g. The raising of Lazarus (11:1-44)
    h. The Sanhedrin's decision concerning Jesus' death (11:45-57)
    i. The anointing of Jesus in Bethany (12:1-8)
    j. Jesus' entry into Jerusalem (12:9-19)
    k. The Greeks and the hour of the Son of man (12:20-50)

Ch. 7:1-13, a strange passage hardly understandable by itself, corresponds to ch. 2:1-12. In both passages Jesus is called upon by his relatives to do something that he refuses to do, giving as his reason: "My hour has not yet come!" Nevertheless, he later does it. Both passages have an introductory function for their respective sections (chs. 2—6 and chs. 7—12). The differences between them are to be explained by their relationship to their respective sections. Jesus' brothers ask him in 7:1-13 to step out in the open with his activity by going to the feast in Jerusalem. When Jesus does go despite his initial refusal, it indicates that he is going to appear publicly at Jerusalem in a manner entirely different from what his brothers intended. It was to be through his suffering and death. The end of this section (12:20-50) points precisely to this.

There were men from Greece who came wanting to see him, and now Jesus replied: "My hour has come." The Greeks (as representatives of the international world) were to see him but in a different way from what they had supposed. They were to be witnesses of his being "lifted up," i.e., his death on the cross. At the beginning of his path towards death the hour had now come, which had not yet come in 2:1-12 and 7:1-13.

As the introduction (7:1-13) has already indicated, the deeds and words of Jesus in chs. 7—12 were performed and spoken in light of the death that awaited him. His very first utterance begins in this way: "Why do you seek to kill me?" he says (7:19). Many extremely varied opinions about Jesus now become known, varying from those of the authorities who wish to render him harmless, to those of the people who believe in him, simply because of his miracles. In the midst of all this Jesus invites everyone: "If any one thirst, let him come to me and drink" (v. 37). He desires to bring life to his enemies as well as his friends, setting forth no demands. Instead he has something to grant which they all need. At the end of the chapter Nicodemus again appears (vv. 50-52), interceding on behalf of Jesus. The words Jesus had spoken to him had not been in vain, even though he did not become one of his disciples. Besides Nicodemus there were the servants who were supposed to arrest Jesus. They were so affected by his words that they did not carry out their assault.

After the narrative of the adulterous woman (8:1-11) (which is obviously an insertion) comes Jesus' long discourse concerning the light of the world (8:12-59). Jesus offers the gift of his Father, when he says: "I am the light of the world." But he is no longer able to make himself comprehensible to his opponents by this comment. It is only after his death that they are going to realize that God had been at work in him (8:28). In his discourse that now follows (8:30-59) concerning Abraham's true descendants, in which Jesus disputes with his opponents, the opposition becomes more and more radical. At last they want to stone him.

In this situation Jesus again performs a miracle, healing a blind man (ch. 9). In an intense and vividly dramatic manner this act of healing, which occurred on the Sabbath, brings the opposition to a new climax. It does so, however, in such a manner that all involved in the event take their fixed positions, and the vast diversity expressed in the words spoken in this chapter by various persons makes clear the division of opinion caused by what Jesus had done. There are the neighbors, the onlookers, the parents, the Pharisees, and the blind man himself, who amid the confusion of opinions is only able to hold on to what he had experienced: "Whether he is a sinner, I do not know," he says; "one thing I know, that though I was blind, now I see" (9:25).

Next comes the story about the good shepherd (ch. 10),* the background of which is the ancient royal assertion that the king is a shepherd of his people, providing them as such with blessing and protection. That the phrase "I am," used here by Jesus, should cause offense is understandable, and so there is another attempt to eliminate him.

The raising of Lazarus in ch. 11, which leads directly to the Passion story, has a powerfully symbolic character. It terminates with the final "I am" phrase: "I am the resurrection and the life" (v. 25). Here in advance is an announcement concerning the significance of Jesus' death and resurrection for those who stand under the dominion of death. He is the one who breaks through the limitations of death for all who believe in him.

The story of the Passion, which agrees with the Synoptic version, begins with the Sanhedrin's decision regarding Jesus' death and it is continued in the account of his anointing at Bethany (12:1-8) and entry into Jerusalem (12:9-19). It is then once more interrupted by the passage (12:20-50), concluding chs. 7—12, and by the farewell discourses in chs. 13—17. In 12:20-50 the Gethsemane narrative is recorded in a way that contrasts sharply with the Synoptic account (cf. vv. 27-31). Its object here is to indicate that Jesus with full assurance and complete assent went to his death as the goal of his activity. He says: "I, when I am lifted up from the earth, will draw all men to myself" (v. 32). "Lifted up" here has a double meaning, viz., as an elevation upon the cross and exaltation to the Father. The comment about the grain of wheat in response to the Greeks (12:24) says the same thing.

Once again Jesus is asked. "Who is this Son of man?" He can only respond by referring to the statement pertaining to impenitence in Isa. 6 (John 13:40. Cf. Isa. 6:9-10. The same comment is found in the last chapter of Acts).

---

*The order of the text is disturbed in this chapter.

4. "But as many as received him" (The Farewell Discourses) (13:1—17:26)

Two actions that Jesus executes for his disciples provide a framework around his Farewell Discourses: the footwashing at the beginning and the highpriestly prayer at the end. In a narrower sense these discourses thus comprise only chs. 14—16: ch. 14, which is concerned with Jesus' farewell, ch. 15 with his abiding, and ch. 16 with the future of the church.

    a. The footwashing ceremony (13:1-30)
        (1) Love to the very end (13:1)
        (2) Jesus washes the disciples' feet (13:3-10)
        (3) The significance of the act (13:12-20)
        (4) The betrayer (13:2, 11, 21-30)
        (5) Jesus' glorification and the new commandment (13:31-35)
        (6) Peter (13:36-38)

The order of events in the Synoptic account of the Passion lies at the basis of this chapter also. The account of the footwashing takes the place of the Last Supper, including the designation of the betrayer and the announcement concerning Peter's denial. These events are here merged into one action (mentioned at the beginning) which Jesus performs for his disciples. This was his demonstration of love for his own to the very end, a love in which the Son of man is glorified and God is glorified in him, as stated at the close (ch. 17). This love is portrayed symbolically in the ceremony of the footwashing, signifying the work of Christ simply for his own, a work that attains completion in his death.

Before the clause that mentions glorification is the statement: "And it was night!" It is the final sentence designating the betrayer. At this point one is reminded of the passage in the Prologue: "The light shines in the darkness, and the darkness has not overcome it" (1:5). The glorification of Christ begins where the darkness has become the greatest, viz., in his betrayal by his own disciples.

The act of footwashing establishes a new manner of community in which the Lord performs the most menial service. Those to whom this service has been done become in it and through it brothers. In this act of their Master a new commandment of love is established.

 b. Jesus' farewell (14:1-31)
  (1) The way to the house of the Father (14:1-14)
  (2) I come to you—in the Counselor (14:15-26)
  (3) The conclusion: the gift of peace, joy in farewell (14:27-31)

In the concluding paragraph of this chapter the two preceding sections are summarized in v. 28: "You heard me say to you, 'I go away (vv. 1-14), and I will come again'" (vv. 15-26). The paradox of Jesus' parting from the disciples is herein intimated. He leaves them; but since he is going to the Father, he will approach them in a new way. This is what he means by the Counselor (or Advocate or Intercessor=Paraclete*) who can come to the disciples only when Jesus goes to the Father. In the final paragraph he says the same thing in different words: he leaves his peace with his disciples (cf. 16:33). The final sentence in v. 31, summoning them to leave the table, indicates that the order of the sections in chs. 14—16 has been confused; for ch. 14:27-31 was obviously intended as a conclusion to the farewell discourses.

 c. Christ's community in the world (John 15—16)
  (1) The vine: Abide in me! (15:1-8)
  (2) The fruit: Abide in my love! (15:9-17)
  (3) The hatred of the world (15:18—16:4)
  (4) The Counselor (16:5-15)
   (a) "I will send the Counselor to you!" (16:5-7)
   (b) He will judge the world (16:8-11)
   (c) "He will guide you into all the truth" (16:12-15)
  (5) The sorrow and joy of departure (16:16-22)

---

*Translator's Note: This term for the Holy Spirit (based on the Greek *paraklētos*) occurs only in the writings of John (4 times in the Gospel—14:16, 26; 15:26; 16:7 and once in the first epistle—2:1). The Greek form is a passive, (from the verb *parakalein* "to call to one's side"). It was a legal term used in the first century Greek mainly of advocates, defenders, or intercessors in reference to legal counsel or witnesses. The term thus describes one who stands by one's side in adversity.

(6) Prayer in the name of Jesus (16:23-28)
(7) Peace amid anguish (16:29-33)

The introductory illustration of the vine sets the tone for this entire section of the farewell discourses. It gives expression to the promise that the disciples will remain in continuous union with Jesus. The church will have life only by abiding in him. Only in this way will it be able to bear fruit; only in this way will it be sheltered from the hatred of the world.

The new presence of Jesus through the Counselor will be effective outwardly as well as inwardly. The church will not need to fear the enmity of the world, because its Advocate will judge the world. The church also will not need to cling to the past for its own life, because the Counselor will go before it, guiding it into all the truth.

With this comment the farewell address again returns to the paradox of Jesus' farewell (16:16-22). The period after his parting will be distinguished by a consciousness of his nearness as well as remoteness. "A little while and you will see me no more," he says, "and again a little while and you will see me." There will be sorrow and joy for the church, but ultimately there will be joy, for he says: "You will see me again." For the period when he is far off there remains to his church the possibility of prayer in Jesus' name (16:23-28). No rule is imposed on the church. The profession of faith on the part of the disciples at this hour of Jesus' departure will not be of long duration (vv. 29-32) and the conclusion of the matter lies in this: "In the world you have tribulation," but "the Lord leaves to his own the peace for which he strove and attained" (v. 33).

   d. Jesus' prayer for his own (17:1-26)
      (1) The request that the Father will glorify him (17:1-5)
      (2) The Son renders an account to the Father (17:6-8, 12-14, 18-19)
      (3) The request that his own be preserved (17:9-11, 15-17)
      (4) The request for the unity of the church (17:20-23)
      (5) The request that the church be perfected
         (17:24-26; cf. 14:1-3)

After leaving his disciples Jesus gives his work on earth back into the hands of his Father. He renders an account concerning his earthly work and then asks the Father to maintain his work and bring it to completion. He has manifested to men the name of God. Because this name is one, and the Son is the one Word of the Father, it is essential for the preservation of his work among men that "they all be one." Upon this unity of the church the missionary efficacy of the church is dependent—"so that the world may believe that thou hast sent me." The final words revert to the beginning of the farewell discourses: the Son asks the Father that he may again be united with his own followers.

D. THE WORD BECAME FLESH (John 18—21)

1. Jesus' suffering and death (18—19)

    a. The arrest of Jesus (18:1-12)
    b. Before the high priest. Peter's denial (18:13-27)
    c. Jesus before Pilate (18:28-40)
    d. Scourging and mockery (Ecce homo!) (19:1-5)
    e. The condemnation (19:6-16)
    f. The crucifixion (19:17-24)
    g. Mary and John (19:25-27)
    h. The death of Jesus (19:28-37)
    i. His burial (19:38-42)

Along with numerous other distinctive features the thing most characteristic of the Passion story in John occurs in the conversations between Pilate and Jesus (18:33-38; 19:4-5, 7-11). These conversations are concerned with Jesus' claim to messiahship.

Pilate asks Jesus: "Are you the king of the Jews?" Jesus' initial response is: "My kingship is not of this world." His second answer, however, reveals the paradoxical character of this royal claim. For he says: "Yes, I am a king. For this I was born, and for this I have come into the world, to bear witness to the truth." This intimate association of the two statements is at first incomprehensible. The relationship is to be explained only by reference to the Old Testament.

Jesus' initial response to Pilate is an explanation of his kingship as that of the king of the final age, the king looked for in Old Testament times. This kingship is "not of this world." The second answer, however, equates this kingship with the prophetic office, described in the second clause, a clause that is meaningless in relationship to the office of king. Jesus as the Servant of the Lord unites in his person both these mediatorial offices of the old covenant.

The question of Pilate: "What is truth?" fades away; the conversation lapses into silence. It is only remotely continued once in Pilate's cry: "Ecce homo!" (Behold the man) and then in Jesus' final reply to Pilate's question: "Where are you from?" At first Jesus was silent, but then after this second question of Pilate he alludes to the Father, from whom the governor has his power, and by whose will the Son is to suffer. In this second part of the conversation with Pilate the concept of the Suffering Servant is added to that of the king and the prophet, although there is but a remote suggestion of this. It is the most comprehensive and profound word of the evangelist in reference to the work of Jesus and is concluded (again only by way of suggestion) in the discussion concerning the inscription on the cross (19:19-22).

2. The Resurrection (John 20—21)

- a. The empty tomb (20:1-10)
- b. Jesus' appearance before Mary Magdalene (20:11-18)
- c. Before the disciples. The gift of the Holy Spirit (20:19-23)
- d. Doubting Thomas (20:24-29)
- e. The conclusion of the book (20:30-31)
- f. Jesus' appearance by the Sea of Tiberias (21:1-14)
- g. His word to Peter (21:15-19)
- h. The disciple whom Jesus loved (21:20-23)
- i. The second ending of the book (21:24-25)

Even as the resurrection accounts in each of the Synoptics are almost always unique even to the story of the empty tomb, so John also exhibits at this point striking peculiarities. Characteristic is the narrative of doubting Thomas in 20:24-29, and the sequel to ch. 21

as a whole. The first narrative concludes with the comment: "Blessed are those who have not seen and yet believe" (20:29). This is a word to the church for whom there would be no other means of approach to Jesus' resurrection except through the testimony of those mentioned in the Gospel. The uncertainty of Thomas is not reprimanded by his exalted Lord. Instead he helps lead him to faith. Those who are like Thomas should hear this.

Behind 21:1-14 is the narrative of Peter's catch of fish (Luke 5:1-11). This appearance of the Resurrected One is intended to show the disciples that their Lord remains with them in his majestic miraculous power as well as in the simple fellowship (vv. 12-13), through which he had shared their life.

A special word is issued now again to Peter (matching that of Matt. 16:17 ff.). To the one who had thrice denied him, the Lord thrice directs the question: "Do you love me?" Then in spite of this he entrusts him with his flock. Peter will not be able indeed to lead the flock by his own strength, but he will become worthy of following Christ, an act which is to be climaxed by death on behalf of his Lord.

In conclusion, there is the obscure comment concerning the disciple "whom Jesus loved." Between him and Peter there were apparently tensions in the first Christian community. One thing is evident, however, the will of the Lord shows to both the way they are to go. In the second ending of the book the Gospel of John is attributed to this disciple (21:24). The first conclusion states why it had been written: "That you may believe that Jesus is the Christ, the Son of God, and that believing you may have life in his name" (20:31).

VI

The Acts of the Apostles

Acts is the second part of a historical work that begins with the Gospel according to St. Luke. It intends to present the course followed by the word of God from Jerusalem to Rome, i.e., the proclamation of the saving work of Jesus Christ on behalf of the whole world. It gives an account of that which was proclaimed by the departing Lord to his disciples in 1:8: "But you shall receive power when the Holy Spirit has come upon you [ch. 2]; and you shall be my witnesses in Jerusalem and in all Judea [chs. 3–7], and Samaria [ch. 8], and to the end of the earth [chs. 9–28]." This resumé presents essentially the plan of Acts.

After Jesus had left his disciples (ch. 1), an event that links Acts with the Gospels, the account of that which was to happen, is initiated by the Pentecost event (ch. 2). Persecution, however, arose concurrently with the sudden spread of the gospel, starting with the receiving of the Holy Spirit. Ridicule (2:13) led to violent interference; and so from Peter and John's initial arrest (4:1-4) and on, there is a chain of persecutions, dispersions, and executions, extending throughout the entire narrative to the last comment in ch. 28. Here Acts concludes with the statement that Paul despite his arrest was preaching the gospel "unhindered."

In the structure of Acts the Stephen section (chs. 6–7) is indeed intended to indicate that the persecution of the Christians, which broke out in Jerusalem following Stephen's murder, was the direct cause of a breakthrough in the proclamation of the gospel to the heathen (chs. 8–12). It was as a result of the flight of Christians from their persecutors that the path of missions, first to Samaria

63

(ch. 8), then to Antioch (ch. 11), became the basis for Paul's missionary ventures.

The second part of Acts (chs. 13–28) gives an account of this enterprise: first, the three missionary journeys, in which Paul traveled as a free man, although persecuted constantly, then the routes taken by Paul the prisoner from Jerusalem by way of Caesarea toward Rome. Here the account breaks off without saying anything more about the legal proceedings against Paul and what later happened to him.

It should be added that Acts does not simply provide information concerning the progress of the proclamation of the word, but expression is also given to the proclamation itself in the many apostolic addresses from the Pentecost sermon of Peter (ch. 2) to the final defense of Paul before Agrippa (ch. 26). With these addresses the two principal types of discourse are also designated: mission sermons that call for an acceptance of the message, and speeches of defense before a court of justice, concerned solely with this message.

The plan of Acts is as follows:

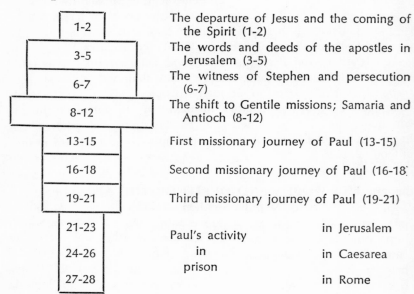

1-2	The departure of Jesus and the coming of the Spirit (1-2)
3-5	The words and deeds of the apostles in Jerusalem (3-5)
6-7	The witness of Stephen and persecution (6-7)
8-12	The shift to Gentile missions; Samaria and Antioch (8-12)
13-15	First missionary journey of Paul (13-15)
16-18	Second missionary journey of Paul (16-18)
19-21	Third missionary journey of Paul (19-21)
21-23	Paul's activity in prison — in Jerusalem
24-26	in Caesarea
27-28	in Rome

A. ASCENSION OF JESUS AND PENTECOST (Acts 1—2)

The preamble addressed to Theophilus (1:1-3) draws upon Luke 1:1-4 and links that which follows directly with the final chapters of the Gospel. The ascension of Jesus (1:4-14) is not depicted as a miraculous exhibition but rather as Jesus' departure from his disciples. The final words of the One who is leaving define in a proclamatory way the course the message is to take from Jerusalem "to the end of the earth." The words of the angel after Jesus' departure point over and beyond his leaving to his return (1:8, 11).

The way in which Judas had to be replaced in order to complete the number twelve for the apostles (1:15-26) also links Acts (as does 1:4-14) with the Gospel; Matthias is appointed to this position by lot.

The Pentecost event (2:1-13) opens the way for the message concerning Christ by breaking the language barrier. It points back to the conclusion of the Primeval history in Gen. 11.* The sermon of Peter (2:14-36) interprets the outpouring of the Spirit as a realization of the prophecy of Joel; and the activity, death, and resurrection of Jesus as a fulfillment of the Messiah who was promised in the Old Testament. "Let all the house of Israel therefore know assuredly that God has made him both Lord and Christ, this Jesus whom you crucified" (2:36), Peter declares.

The result of the Pentecost event and Peter's sermon was that a great multitude of people asked "What shall we do?" and the response was the baptism of many people (2:37-41). The first congregation, which originated in this way, is portrayed in its communal life. This extended even to the sharing of possessions, in prayer, in celebration of the Lord's Supper, and in joyful praise of God (2:42-47).

B. THE WORDS AND DEEDS OF THE APOSTLES IN JERUSALEM (3—5)

1. The healing of the lame man by Peter (3:1-11)
2. Peter's sermon (3:12-26)
3. The arrest of Peter and John (4:1-4)

---

*Cf. Westermann, *op. cit.*, p. 28.

The persecution of the Christians begins in this second division. Ch. 3 presents two examples of the activity and utterances of the apostles. Violent reaction then set in: Peter and John were arrested (4:1-4). At the trial the next day the judge was unable to accomplish anything. The healing of the lame man gave evidence of the apostles' authority. Thus they were able to confess their faith in the resurrected Christ before their judges, declaring: "There is salvation in no one else; for there is no other name under heaven, given among men by which we must be saved" (4:12). It was impossible to keep them from speaking. "For we cannot but speak of what we have seen and heard," was their reply (4:20). The Christian community returned thanks to God for their release. Their prayer caused the gift of the Spirit to be extended also to others. Thus the use of force simply led to fresh outspoken proclamation (4:23-31).

At this point a second description of the first congregation follows, corresponding to that of 2:42-47. It shows how the church existed, expanding in size despite persecutions (4:32-37). How intense this existence was is indicated by the horrifying story that tells about the punishment of two people who intended to deceive the congregation. This recalls the story of Achan's theft in Josh. 7.

The miracles and preaching of the apostles continue (5:12-16). Again follow imprisonment, release, and confession of faith before the Jewish judicial authorities (5:17-42). This time it was the advice of the Pharisee Gamaliel to which they were indebted for their release.

C. THE WITNESS OF STEPHEN AND THE PERSECUTION
(Acts 6—7)

1. The selection of the seven deacons (6:1-7)
2. The arrest of Stephen (6:8-15)

3. His speech of defense: a review of God's history with his people (7:1-53)
4. The stoning of Stephen (7:54-60)

In chs. 1—3 the community continues to live unmolested; in chs. 4—5 there is a beginning of persecution. Nevertheless, all the arrests terminate in miraculous release. In chs. 6—7, however, the situation becomes grimly serious; for the arrest of Stephen is followed by his execution.

As the church grows, new ministerial offices become necessary (6:1-7). The Book of Acts comments on the deacons, however, not because of their official position but in order to report that those who held this new office were really fundamentally witnesses of Jesus Christ. Because Stephen aroused the wrath of the authorities as such a witness, he was arrested (6:8-15), and it was as a witness to Christ that he was also stoned (7:54-60). The lengthy sermon of Stephen (7:1-53) unfolds the story of salvation from Abraham to Solomon. Up to that point his judges had to give assent to every word. It was only in his concluding utterances that he accused his judges. "You have murdered the One of whom the prophets spoke," he told them, "even as your fathers persecuted and murdered the prophets" (7:51-53). His final word, however, was a prayer for the forgiveness of those who were stoning him (7:60).

It should be noted that the history of God's people in Stephen's address is presented without any attempt to provide a new Christian interpretation.

D. THE SHIFT TO GENTILE MISSIONS:
SAMARIA AND ANTIOCH (Acts 8—12)

1. The persecution of the church, especially by Saul (8:1-3)
2. The miracles of Philip in Samaria (8:4-8)
3. Simon the sorcerer (8:9-13)
4. The apostles in Samaria (8:14-25)
5. The minister of the Ethiopian queen (8:26-40)
6. The conversion of Saul (9:1-22)
7. The plot against him by the Jews (9:23-25)
8. Paul in Jerusalem (9:26-31)

9. The miracles of Peter in Lydda and Joppa (9:32-45)
10. The baptism of Peter by Cornelius the centurion (10:1-48)
11. His intercession on behalf of Gentile missions (11:1-18)
12. The founding of the church in Antioch. The presence there of Barnabas and Paul (11:19-26)
13. Agabus and the collection on behalf of Jerusalem (11:27-30)
14. The execution of James (12:1-2)
15. The imprisonment and release of Peter (12:3-19)
16. The death of Herod (12:20-23)
17. The increase of the Gospel (12:24)

This part of Acts is significant for the definite progress into which the book sets the events of the first community of believers. It begins with the first extensive persecution of the church (8:1-3) and ends with the sentence: "But the word of God grew and multiplied" (12:24). It was Saul especially who participated in the persecution; but then he himself became a messenger of Christ. It was as a man persecuted by his own people that he assumed a leading role in the extension of the message. Another leader, James, was again put to death (12:1-2), but the death of this witness did not alter the progress of the Gospel in any way.

It is in this section alone that we encounter the activity of several apostles side-by-side: Philip in Samaria, Peter in Lydda and Joppa, Barnabas and finally Paul in Antioch.

The way in which the activity of Peter and Paul is combined in chs. 9—12 is especially noteworthy. Perhaps this association is intended to express the fact that the one as well as the other participated in the progress of the gospel despite the contrasts between them. (In Acts, however, their differences are quite insignificant.)

The underlying theme of this part of Acts, however, is clear. It is the way the message concerning Christ was rapidly extended to the Gentiles. All is recounted with astonishment and awe. The section begins with the activity of Philip in Samaria, a venture expressly endorsed by the apostles (8:4-25). He baptized the Ethiopian minister (8:26-40). The turning point from an illustrative standpoint was in this instance the exposition of Scripture. It was the passage that speaks of the Servant of the Lord, suffering and dying vicariously for the sins of many (Isa. 53).

The second event, leading to Gentile mission work, was the conversion of Paul. In this account the Lord of the church himself issued a call to the one who then became the leading apostle to the Gentiles. The story of this call is later recounted two times more by Paul himself (2:3-21; 26:9-20), not to mention Gal. 1:13-24. The way the same occurrence is freely told in these four accounts, each time with varying details, provides a good example of the freedom from literal interpretation in the biblical narrative.

The third event is Peter's baptism of Cornelius (ch. 10). In his sermon, justifying the baptism of a Gentile (11:1-18), Peter speaks the decisive word on behalf of this transition to Gentile missions—God himself had commanded that this step be taken. It was he who had sent Philip to the road where the Ethiopian minister was reading the Book of Isaiah. He had stood in Paul's way and brought him to conversion. He had sent Peter to Cornelius the centurion, and Peter could only say: "Who was I, that I could withstand God?" (11:17). The dietary laws and the rules concerning purification were a tremendous obstacle to this transition for the Jewish Christians. These stipulations made it impossible for them to eat together with the Gentiles. But the obstacle was removed by God himself in the vision, in which he commanded Peter to eat the unclean animals (10:9-16).

E. PAUL'S MISSIONARY JOURNEYS (Acts 13:1—21:17)*

1. Paul's first missionary journey (13—14)

   a. The mission from Antioch; Cyprus (13:1-5)
   b. The magician and the proconsul (13:6-12)
   c. Paul's sermon and his persecution in Antioch of Pisidia (13:13-52)
   d. In Iconium, Lystra, and Derbe (14:1-20)
   e. The return to Antioch (14:21-28)

At the assembly of the church in Antioch Paul and Barnabas were commissioned for their missionary work (13:1-3). Upon returning they told the congregational assembly "all that God had done with them, and how he had opened a door of faith to the Gentiles (14:21-28). The events that occurred on these journeys

---

*Translator's Note: See map of Paul's missionary journeys (inside back cover).

revolve around the same themes essentially: (1) preaching results
in the acceptance of the message and its rejection; (2) the apostles
provide healing and help, (3) they suffer persecution, slander, and
blows. Sufficient as an illustration is the event that is briefly reported in 14:19 f.—Paul was stoned, dragged out of the city, and
left for dead. "But when the disciples gathered about him, he rose
up and entered the city." On the next day he resumed his missionary journey with Barnabas. The matter-of-fact, almost too prosaic
manner in which such an episode is reported precludes here any
legendary development or exaltation of the apostles.

2. The apostolic council (15:1-33)

    a. The occasion: the requirement of circumcision (15:1-6)
    b. Peter, Paul, and James speak (15:7-21)
    c. The letter to Antioch: the apostolic decree (15:22-33)

The decisions of the apostolic council pose various problems
when one compares Acts 15 with Gal. 2:1-10. It is essential to note
that the Gentile mission of Paul and Barnabas was recognized
without the Gentile Christians having to abide by Jewish laws.
This was in opposition to a group of Jewish Christians. The precepts
that were still retained have been expressed a bit differently in
v. 20 and v. 29 (cf. also 21:25). They were furthermore not retained forever.

3. Paul's second missionary journey (15:35—18:22)

    a. The separation from Barnabas (15:35-40)
    b. From Derbe and Lystra to Troas (16:1-8)
    c. The Macedonian call. The journey as far as Philippi (16:9-12)
    d. Songs of praise from the prison in Philippi (16:13-40)
    e. Thessalonica and Beroea (17:1-15)
    f. In Athens; Paul's address on the Areopagus (17:16-34)
    g. Eighteen months in Corinth (18:1-17)
    h. To Antioch by way of Ephesus and Jerusalem* (18:18-22)

---

*Translator's Note: The reference to Paul's going up and greeting the
church (18:22) implies that he went up to Jerusalem. The German rendering
of the Zurich Bible, followed here by the author, adds the phrase "nach
Jerusalem."

It is said of the original church: "They were of one heart and one soul" (4:32). That this sentence is not meant in an idealistic way, however, is indicated by the argument over technicalities that led to the apostolic council in ch. 15. Another case in point is the personal quarrel between Paul and Barnabas at the beginning of the second missionary journey (15:35-40). The most important event on this second missionary journey was his crossing over to Europe. This change of program was occasioned by Paul's vision, in which he heard the cry: "Come over to Macedonia and help us" (16:9-12). It indicates how Paul understood his mission. The message he had to bring was a response to those who called for help.

The first person in Philippi to turn to the faith was a woman (16:13-15), but persecutions already set in again. A narrative that is especially typical of Acts tells how a jailer became a Christian (16:16-40).

In Athens Paul delivered his so-called Areopagus address* which is distinguished to a great extent by Greek thought (17: 22-34). Many concepts from popular philosophy are found in it, even the quotation from a Greek poet Aratus† (17:28). The address captured the interest of Paul's hearers by its allusion to the altar inscription: "To an unknown god."

In Corinth Paul remained a longer time, earning his living by means of his trade (18:3). Particularly emphasized during this sojourn in Corinth is the way he transferred his work from the Jews who rejected him to the Gentiles (18:4-7). Because of Jewish persecution he then had to move on (18:18-22).

4. Paul's third missionary journey (18:23—21:17)

    a. Galatia and Phrygia: Apollos in Ephesus (18:23-28)
    b. The disciples of John the Baptist and Ephesus (19:1-7)
    c. Paul's activity in Ephesus (19:8-20)

---

*Translator's Note: Areopagus was a hill in Athens, opposite the Acropolis. It was the site of a famous court. Areopagus means literally "hill of Ares (Lat. Mars)" (cf. A. V. Acts 17:22).

†Translator's Note: "For we are indeed his offspring." This is to be found in Aratus, *Phaenomenon*. The other quotation: "For in him we live and move and have our being" has been attributed to Epimenides, one of the seven sages of Greece (7th cent. B.C.).

   d. The decision to journey to Jerusalem and to Rome (19:21-22)
   e. The revolt of Demetrius, the silversmith (19:23-40)
   f. The continuation of the journey; sojourn in Troas (Eutychus) (20:1-16)
   g. Farewell at Miletus (20:17-38)
   h. The journey via Tyre and Caesarea to Jerusalem (21:1-17)
       The prophet Agabus (vv. 10-14. Cf. 11:27-30).

The initial stage of this journey (18:23—19:7) indicates that there existed at that time widely-distributed congregations which observed John's baptism. A number of them had joined Christian congregations along with their leader Apollos.

The account of Paul's long activity in Ephesus provides a vivid impression of the turbulent religious life of the Hellenistic cities. At that time there were exorcists who drove out demons and used for this purpose names that were most in vogue just then (19: 13-20). There was a whole trade that profited from a local cult of Artemis.* When one group wanted to get rid of another group, it was possible to bring the city into an uproar. Everyone would run and scream without knowing really what it was all about. The tiny and impotent Christian congregation in the midst of all this had to seek its way. Though shoved and pushed aside, scorned and wrongfully accused, it nevertheless continued to increase and advance.

In the portrayal of the third missionary journey it is especially noteworthy that the continuous record of the trip includes only brief notes concerning the stations along the way.† In between are inserted little episodes that have no relationship to one another. Thus there has been inserted into the record of the journey (20: 1-16) a little scene (vv. 7-12) that sheds a bright light on the profound and genuine humanity that was a part of the progress of Christ's message into the world. Even during an earth-shaking sermon of Paul it could happen that a young man fell asleep, because

---

   *Translator's Note: Artemis was the chief female deity in Ephesus. As the mother goddess, the emblem of fertility, she was worshiped throughout Asia Minor. Her temple was one of the seven wonders of the ancient world.

   †They are expressed partly in the "we" form in passages that originate perhaps with the physician Luke.

the service lasted too long. And it was then Paul himself who cared for the youth and restored him again to life.

This human trait also distinguished Paul's farewell sermon at Miletus, where he had summoned the elders from Ephesus. One might compare it sometime to the farewell address of Samuel in 1 Sam. 12. In 21:10-14 there is again a little individual scene that gives a picture of early Christian prophecy.

F. PAUL'S ACTIVITY AS A PRISONER (Acts 21:18—28:31)

1. Paul as a prisoner in Jerusalem (21:18—23:35)

a. Paul's report before James and his agreement with him (21:18-26)
b. The riot. Protective custody provided by the cohort (21:27-40)
c. Paul's address in his own defense at the gateway of the barracks (22:1-22)
d. Paul's appeal to his Roman citizenship (22:23-29)
e. The tribune sets Paul before the Sanhedrin (22:30)
f. Tumult within the Sanhedrin (23:1-11)
g. The foiling of the conspiracy (23:12-22)
h. Paul taken in escort to Felix the governor of Caesarea (23:23-55)

From this point to the end there is a continuous account of Paul's destiny, narrated with restraint and dispassion. Nowhere is there an exaggeration or overemphasis. In just this way the progress of a prisoner who was hated, flogged, and fanatically persecuted is turned into a quiet triumphal procession. In this connection, however, it was not Paul but his Lord who was the victor.

The beginning of the account reveals in an alarming way that Paul was received by the Jewish Christians in Jerusalem only with deep suspicion even as before (21:18-26). His persecution by the Jews, which began at once (21:27-40), is strikingly reminiscent of the arrest of Jesus. Now as then they wanted the death of the one whom they considered to be a traitor to their faith. Paul's arrest by the Roman cohort saved his life. One senses, however, what little concern Paul had for his life and the great concern he had for his message. This is shown by the way he turned in front of the gateway of the barracks to speak to these people who had beaten him and wanted to take his life. He delivered his address of defense (21:1-22). At the conclusion, however, they again sought his death (22:22).

The Roman commandant, as at the time of Jesus' arrest, was at a loss what to do. He wanted to force Paul into an admission of guilt by flogging him, but at this point Paul appealed to his Roman citizenship (22:23-29). Thus the commandant had to send him to a higher court of justice, after a trial before the high priest (23: 1-11) foundered.

2. Paul as prisoner in Caesarea (24:1—26:32)

- a. Paul before Felix responds to his accusers (24:1-21)
- b. Felix protects the prisoner (24:22-27)
- c. Paul appeals to the emperor (25:1-12)
- d. Festus makes a report and brings Paul forward (25:13-27)
- e. The address of Paul before Agrippa (26:1-29)
- f. Agrippa confirms Paul's innocence (26:30-32)

The Jews in their ineffective hatred against Paul retreat gradually into the background in these three chapters in a way that is strange and profoundly moving in the light of subsequent development. Their accusations against Paul die away before the quiet and just authority of the Romans. The representatives of this power, on the other hand, merge in clear-cut profile. They are portrayed vividly and sympathetically. The forum for the proceedings against Paul, "the ringleader of the sect of the Nazarenes" (24:5) is shifted inconspicuously from the Jewish to the Roman court of justice, which decides the case quite justly. All in turn come to the conclusion that the point of issue against Paul was not a crime worthy of death. At the same time one senses in the narratives that the representatives of the Roman governmental authority were quietly beginning to take a personal interest in the message for which Paul was risking so much. The victorious advance of the gospel in the Roman world is thus intimated.

The address of Paul before Festus and Agrippa (ch. 26) is in an intense, almost dramatic narrative. Before these two men there passes in review the account of how a law-abiding Jew, a zealous persecutor of Christians, encountered the exalted Lord of the Christian church, who had given him his commission. It was in the fulfillment of this commission that he now stood before these two representatives of Roman power. In this speech Paul declares in simple, quite personal language that he did not look upon the two men before him simply as the government. He desired and prayed God that they also might some day become Christians (26:29).

3. Paul on the journey to Rome (27:1—28:31)

a. The voyage from Caesarea to Crete (27:1-13)
b. The storm at sea and the rescue (27:14-44)
c. The sojourn at Malta (28:1-10)
d. Continued journey and arrival at Rome (28:11-16)
e. Paul as a prisoner in Rome (28:17-31)

The unusually detailed "we" account (written here surely by an eyewitness) depicts the apostle Paul as a man who was entirely resigned to his situation and concerned about the people in the little group to which he now belonged. He provided for their welfare with complete disregard as to whether they were Christian or pagan. Thus he gave good advice at the outset concerning the ship voyage (27:9 ff.). Then he maintained a calm assurance in a most serious peril at sea, when the others had already given up hope of rescue. He was able to encourage them (27:20-26). Thus he rescued the entire ship in a critical moment (27:27-32), exhorting those numb with desperation to take some nourishment again.

This picture has significance for the further progress of Christianity in the world. Paul spoke to the despairing, "and when he had said this, he took bread, and giving thanks to God in the presence of all, he broke it and began to eat" (27:35). Then he helped the father of the official on the island of Malta, where the shipwrecked passengers found refuge, and he healed many other people after this (28:1-10). It is as though it must again be made emphatically clear, now before Paul's arrival in Rome and the then impending drama, that the Savior was coming to mankind in the gospel, the Savior who desired to help them in all their trouble. Paul was the messenger of this gospel.

Paul was permitted to stay in Rome under guard in a dwelling of his own. He also had the opportunity to continue his effectiveness, employing it again with the Jews one last time, as he attempted to make it clear to them: "It is because of the hope of Israel that I am bound with this chain" (28:20). He could only tell them that their hardness of heart had already been proclaimed by the prophet Isaiah (6:9 f.) and that salvation therefore had now passed to the Gentiles (28:17-28). And so Acts closes with Paul "preaching the kingdom of God and teaching about the Lord Jesus Christ quite openly and unhindered" (28:30).

Part Two

PAULINE EPISTLES

VII

The Letter to the Romans

The Letter to the Romans was written by Paul probably in the winter of 55-56 A.D. in Corinth, as he was preparing for his visit to Jerusalem. He wanted to deliver there the offering he had collected in his congregations for Jerusalem (cf. 2 Cor. 8—9). After this he wanted to do missionary work in the western part of the Roman empire, even as far as Spain, and on his way there to visit Rome.

There already was a congregation in Rome, founded by unknown Christians. Normally Paul held to the principle that he would only preach the gospel where there was still no Christian church. But he needed the support of the Roman congregation for his missionary work in the west. He expected assistance from them on his way to Spain (15:23 f., 28) and wanted now to introduce himself to the congregation in his letter. Thus in the Letter to the Romans we are caught up immediately in the progress of the gospel "to the ends of the earth." The message that is unfolded in it is the irresistible power (1:16) that impels its messengers to go to the ends of the earth then known to them.

Since the situation of the Letter to the Romans was a special one, it was not necessary for Paul to write it in response to questions, requests, and problems of this church to whom he was writing, as he does in his other letters. Completely free of this responsibility, he could rather develop the message concerning Jesus Christ, even as he proclaimed it. For this reason the Letter to the Romans has a clear, discernible structure. It unfolds the message that Paul is bringing even as he formulates it as his confession (1:16 f.) at the beginning. A comparison of the plan of Romans with that

79

of the hymn* in which Luther set forth the message of the Reformation indicates this:

The Letter to the Romans	**Dear Christians, one and all, rejoice**
"I am not ashamed of the gospel" (1:16 f.)	(1) Dear Christians, one and all, rejoice, With exultation springing, And, with united heart and voice And holy rapture singing, **Proclaim the wonders God hath done** How His right arm the victory won; Right dearly it hath cost Him.
Gentiles and Jews under the wrath of God (1:18—3:20)	(2) **Fast bound in Satan's chains I lay,** Death brooded darkly o'er me, Sin was my torment night and day, In sin my mother bore me; Yea, deep and deeper still I fell, Life had become a living hell, So firmly sin possessed me.
	(3) **My own good works availed me naught,** No merit they attaining; Free will against God's judgment fought, Dead to all good remaining. My fears increased till sheer despair Left naught but death to be my share; The pangs of hell I suffered.
Now is revealed the righteousness which comes by faith in Jesus Christ (3:21—8:39)	(4) **But God beheld my wretched state** Before the world's foundation, And, mindful of His mercies great, He planned my soul's salvation. A father's heart He turned to me, Sought my redemption fervently: He shared His dearest Treasure.

---

*Translator's Note: This is the first congregational hymn that Luther wrote. It was written in 1523 and appeared in *Das Achtliederbuch,* the first hymnbook of the Reformation, published in Nürnberg in 1523. Inasmuch as the hymn is not well known in English, it has been quoted in its entirety in the slightly altered translation of Richard Massie in his *Martin Luther's Spiritual Songs* (1854), as it appears in *The Lutheran Hymnal* (Concordia Publishing House, 1941). The phrases singled out by the author as comparable to the development of Paul's thought have been indicated in bold type.

(5) He spoke to His beloved Son:
  'Tis time to have compassion.
 Then go, bright Jewel of My crown,
  And bring to man salvation;
 From sin and sorrow set him free,
 Slay bitter death for him that he
  May live with Thee forever.

(6) **The Son obeyed His Father's will,**
  Was born of virgin mother,
 And God's good pleasure to fulfill,
  He came to be my Brother,
 No garb or pomp or power He wore,
 A servant's form, like mine, He bore,
  To lead the devil captive.

(7) To me He spake: Hold fast to me,
  I am thy Rock and Castle;
 Thy ransom I Myself will be,
  For thee I strive and wrestle;
 For I am with thee, I am thine.
 And evermore thou shalt be Mine;
  The Foe shall not divide us.

(8) The Foe shall shed My precious blood,
  Me of My life bereaving.
 All this I suffer for thy good
  Be steadfast and believing.
 Life shall from death the victory win,
 My innocence shall bear thy sin;
  So art thou blest forever.

(9) Now to My Father I depart,
  The Holy Spirit sending,
 And, heavenly wisdom to impart,
  My help to thee extending.
 He shall in trouble comfort thee,
 Teach thee to know and follow Me,
  And in all truth shall guide thee.

"I appeal to you therefore, brethren, to present your bodies as a living sacrifice . . . which is your spiritual worship" (12:1—15:33)

(10) **What I have done and taught, teach thou,**
  My ways forsake thou never;
 So shall my Kingdom flourish now
  And God be praised forever.
 Take heed lest men with base alloy
  The heavenly treasure should destroy;
  This counsel I bequeath thee.

This Letter to the Romans is not in the first place doctrine but rather a message. Its basic features bear a remote resemblance to those of the Old Testament psalms of thanksgiving; viz., proclamation, introductory summary, a review of dire need, an account of the rescue, a response of the one who has been saved.

An important aspect of Romans of course has not been brought out at all in this sketch. This is the way Paul in his introductory summary (1:16 f.) refers to a passage from the Old Testament: "But the righteous shall live by his faith" (Hab. 2:4). This relationship to the Old Testament and thereby to God's people of the old covenant is manifest throughout the whole letter. The concluding summary of the first section (3:10-18) is documented in detail by quotations from the Old Testament. At the beginning of the second section, the chapter on Abraham (4) points out the primary biblical example of justification by faith. The latter half of the fifth chapter contrasts Adam and Christ; the seventh chapter the life in Christ and the life under the law. This line of thought emerges most prominently in the great parenthetical section (chs. 9–11), where Paul inquires concerning the destiny of Israel.

The main divisions of Romans may be charted as follows:

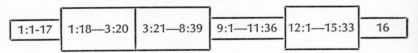

| 1:1-17 | 1:18—3:20 | 3:21—8:39 | 9:1—11:36 | 12:1—15:33 | 16 |

A. THE INTRODUCTION (Romans 1:1-17)

The salutation includes a reference to the sender (v. 1), the address (v. 7a), and a greeting (v. 7b). The reference to the sender is expanded more fully by an initial paraphrase of the gospel (vv. 2-4), whose messenger Paul is (v. 5). It involves also the church in Rome, to whom the letter is directed. Then follows an expression of thanks addressed to God for the faith of the congregation in Rome, whom Paul is longing to visit (vv. 8-15). He wants to come to them with the message (vv. 16 f.) that he is now presenting to them.

PART ONE:

B. GENTILES AND JEWS UNDER GOD'S WRATH
(Romans 1:18—3:20)

1. The Gentiles, who could have known God's will (1:18-32)

2. The Jews, to whom God's will was revealed (2:1—3:8)

3. They are all under the dominion of sin (3:9-20)

The revelation of God's righteousness through faith in Christ *for everyone* (1:16 f.) proves that *all* other ways of salvation are at an end. This Paul demonstrates to the Gentiles and to the Jews. Even the Gentiles could have known God; for his invisible nature has been perceivable ever since the creation. They, however, did not honor him as God, but worshiped instead graven images. Therefore God gave them up to their folly (1:18-32).

But even the Jews, who have relied on the law committed to them and have depended on their belonging to the people of God because of circumcision, are also under God's wrath, inasmuch as they set themselves up as judges over others and yet are doing the same things themselves. "For God shows no partiality" (2:11), Paul declares. Those who sin without the law and those who sin under it are alike before God (2:1—3:8).

Therefore no one can be justified by the works of the law. All are under the dominion of sin, even as Scripture says (3:9-20).

PART TWO:

C. THE GIFT OF JUSTIFICATION (Romans 3:21—8:39)

1. The new message: justified by faith (3:21-31)

2. Abraham, the father of faith (4:1-20)

3. Justification by faith is given to us in Christ (5:1—7:25)

    a. The death of Christ has reconciled us with God (5:1-11)

    b. As through one man sin and death came into the world so through one man came acquittal and life (5:12-21)

    c. We are baptized into Christ's death and rise with him (6:1-11)

    d. Free from sin for the service of righteousness (6:12-23)

   e. Free from sin to become a new spiritual being (7:1-6)
   f. "The commandment which promised life proved to be death to me
       . . . Wretched man that I am" (7:7-25)

4. With justification by faith a new life is given to us (8:1-39)

   a. "Now no condemnation for those who are in Christ" (8:1-11)
   b. We are now children of God and fellow heirs with Christ (8:12-17)
   c. The sufferings of this present time will also no longer separate us
       from the love of God in Jesus Christ (8:18-39)
       (1) The creation waits with eager longing together with us
            (8:18-22)
       (2) We ourselves are saved in hope (8:23-25)
       (3) "The Spirit himself intercedes for us" (8:26-27)
       (4) "In everything God works for good with those who love him"
            (8:28-30)
       (5) "If God is for us who is against us?" (8:31-39)

In this fundamental section of the Letter to the Romans Paul
works out in greater detail the message concerning justification by
faith, which he had put at the beginning of the letter (1:16 f.).
There he had initially formulated it as his confession of faith, and
the primary section which develops this phrase ends again in a
joyous confession (8:31-39). This accords with the fact that Paul
has been speaking almost continuously in the first person in this
central section. Thus theological reflection on and explanation of
justification by faith proceed from confession and end in confession.

This is manifested in an especially forceful way by the transition
from ch. 7 to ch. 8. The seventh chapter, which describes existence
under the law, ends with the cry: "Wretched man that I am! Who
will deliver me from this body of death?" This cry is followed
abruptly by the joyous shout of relief: "Thanks be to God through
Jesus Christ our Lord!"—the joyful cry of one who has been given
the new life. In ch. 8 this life is then described.

For man, standing under God's wrath, i.e., Gentiles and Jews
(1:18–3:20), there remains in the end nothing but that cry of
despair. Christ, however, is God's answer to this lament, and those
who hear the promise concerning him can now in relief and freedom join in the exultant confession of the redeemed (8:31-39).

Since Christ, however, is the answer to the lament of all humanity, imprisoned in the body of death, the liberating message must be carried out into all the world. For this reason Paul had been set apart for the proclamation of the gospel among all the Gentiles (1:1-7). For this reason also he had included the Roman church in the movement of the gospel to the ends of the earth.

The theological and conceptual unfolding of the divine saving act in Christ proceeds from the concept of justification by faith (1:16 f.) to a fundamental thesis, formulated in 3:28: "For we hold that a man is justified by faith apart from the works of law." Paul states this principle in opposition to the Jewish teaching of his time, yet not in opposition to the Old Testament. This he intends to demonstrate in ch. 4. Abraham, he maintains, was justified by God on the basis of his faith (Gen. 15:6), not on the basis of his circumcision (4:9-12), nor on the basis of works (4:13-15). In this way Abraham became the father of those who believe (4:16-25). God has demonstrated the same thing by redeeming us through Christ, showing that Christ died for us while we were yet sinners (5:1-11), in order that we could obtain access to grace and peace with God by faith alone.

This divine act, which is intended for everyone, is so decisive that it stands at the center of world history as the turning point of two epochs. The one epoch, determined by Adam, is dominated by sin and death, occasioned by one man's sin. The other epoch, determined by Christ, is dominated by the gift of an imputed righteousness, produced by one man's act of righteousness (5:12-21). The individual believer participates in this gift by means of baptism. Through it he shares in Christ's death and resurrection. Thus death and sin have dominion over him no longer (6:1-11). With regard to Christian conduct this means an absolute freedom from slavery to sin, a freedom for service to God with one's entire being,* for a "service of righteousness" (6:12-23). There is at the same time a freedom from being bound to the flesh (by the law) and a freedom for a new service in the Spirit (7:1-6).

Paul accounts for this change by contrasting existence under the law (ch. 7) with the life in Christ (ch. 8). Chapter 7 explains

---

*This is dealt with in 12:1 ff.

how the law drives one into captivity of sin and death. In itself the law is good. It ought to lead to life, but inasmuch as it excites covetousness, it results in sin and death. It leads human existence into a desperate and deadly conflict.

Christ has come into this situation and has set us free from the law of sin and death (ch. 8). There is now no longer any condemnation for those who are in Christ (8:1-11). They have received the spirit of sonship, which gives them immediate access to God in calling on him as Father (8:12-17). In the closing portion (8:18-39) the circle is greatly expanded. The salvation provided in Christ does not only extend to the state of captivity under sin but also to the reality of being subject to the suffering in which we participate with all creatures. The whole creation eagerly awaits the final redemption together with the children of God (8:18-22). We ourselves are not removed from suffering but are saved in hope. Yet the Spirit intercedes for us in the afflictions that remain in the present age (8:26-27). Therefore the believer can face anything that may happen to him with a calm assurance: everything must work for his good (8:28-30).

Thus at the end Paul can confess his confidence with jubilant certainty in a manner that is almost hymnlike: "He who did not spare his own Son but gave him up for us all, will he not also give us all things with him?" (Compare the hymn: "In thee is gladness." *)

D. THE QUESTION OF THE DESTINY OF ISRAEL
(Romans 9—11)

1. How deeply concerned Paul was over this problem (9:1-5)
2. The promises remain intact (9:6-13)
3. God has called his new people from the Jews *and* Gentiles. Only a remnant of Israel, however, is present (9:14—10:3)
4. The nearness of the word of faith (10:4-17)
5. Israel has also heard it (10:18-21)
6. Has God then rejected his people? (11:1-16)
7. The branches that were broken off and those that were grafted in (11:17-24)

---

*Translator's Note: A German hymn by Johann Lindemann (d. 1630), translated by Catherine Winkworth for her *Lyra Germanica*. It is included also in her *Chorale Book for England* (1863).

8. "A hardening has come upon a part of Israel until the full number of the Gentiles come in" (11:25-32)
9. How unsearchable are his ways! (11:33-36).

These three chapters are among the most difficult passages in the New Testament to understand. The beginning and conclusion are clear. Paul was moved in his inmost being by the question concerning the destiny of the people of God in the old covenant. He was even willing to be accursed and cut off from Christ, if thereby he could have saved his people (9:3). This personal sense of bewilderment breaks through again at the end of the first section (10:1-3): "My heart's desire and prayer to God for them is that they may be saved." One must realize at the same time that Paul spoke this way concerning those at whose hands he had suffered the most bitter persecutions and whose passionate hatred he had continually encountered!

At the close there are the wonderful words in praise of God, which begin: "O the depth of the riches and wisdom and knowledge of God . . . " Here Paul bows before the inscrutable judgment of God, which he cannot fathom and before which he must also capitulate as far as his own thoughts are concerned. These final words express clearly enough that all Paul's reflective explanations were unable to penetrate the mystery of God's decree regarding the way of his people.

The most important feature in these explanatory comments is the way in which they point beyond the present state of affairs. Although only a remnant of Israel now belongs to the new people of God, this is not God's last word to Israel. Therefore the branches that have been grafted in must not exalt themselves above the ones that have been broken off. The separation between those who have become hardened and those who believe in Christ is not yet the end of God's history with his people.

In the midst of these reflections in 10:4-17 Paul invites those who have stood aloof from the message of Christ. He does so in an unusually beautiful and clear description of how one comes to faith in Christ. It is in the chain that leads from sending out witnesses to preaching, to hearing, to believing, to calling upon the Father. Thus in the midst of this difficult chapter the objective of the primary section is again taken up, viz., the turning in trust of a child to his father (8:15).

E. THE NEW WORSHIP OF GOD (Romans 12:1—15:13)

1. The living sacrifice, the spiritual worship (12:1-2)
2. Members of one body (12:3-8)
3. Admonitions concerning living with one another (12:9-21)
4. "Let every person be subject to the governing authorities" (13:1-7)
5. "Love is the fulfilling of the law" (13:8-10)
6. The day is at hand. Let us awake! (13:11-14)
7. Welcome the weak (14:1-12)
8. Give no offense to your brother (14:13-23)
9. The strong ought to uphold the weak (15:1-6)
10. "Welcome one another" (15:7-12)
11. The benediction of peace (15:13)

The numerous admonitions in the closing part of Romans may be best perceived by means of the two paragraphs that bind it to the primary section. The first is the exhortation: "I appeal to you by the mercies of God" (12:1)*—an admonition to understand the new life in Christ as the new worship of God. The second is the paragraph concerning "knowing what hour it is," because the night is gone and the day is at hand (13:11-14)—hence the admonition to conduct oneself becomingly as in the day.

Section One: Spiritual Worship (12—13)

The reason that admonitions of a cultic-sacral type are entirely lacking in this final section in a notable way is the fact that the new life of the Christian is thought of as a divine service, as a living sacrifice. The public worship of the congregation is accomplished by the way its members conduct themselves in the world. For this, however, it is essential that the congregation be one body in Christ and that believers know themselves to be members of this body, each with his own gifts (cf. 12:3-8; 1 Cor. 12—14). This concept is developed in a large number of individual admonitions (12:9-21), proceeding from the clause: "Let love be genuine" and

---

*Chapters 3-8 are summarized in this phrase "mercies of God."

ending in the sentence: "Therefore love is the fulfilling of the law" (13:8-10). In between is the admonition to obedience over against authority (13:1-7).

Section Two: The New Life in Christ (14:1—15:13)

This section has to do essentially with one evidence of the new life in Christ: the amicable living together of the strong and the weak, i.e., those who realize themselves to be still strongly bound to tradition and those for whom it now has no more significance. Paul does not take sides but warns the one against judging and the other against despising (14:1-12).

In the midst of this admonition is his profound observation concerning the new life of Christ: "None of us lives to himself, and none of us dies to himself. If we live, we live to the Lord, and if we die, we die to the Lord; so then, whether we live or whether we die, we are the Lord's" (14:7 f.). As far as this new life is concerned it is more important not to give offense to a brother than to insist on one's own principles (14:13-23). The strong in this connection are especially obliged to assist the weak (15:1-6).

Even as Paul placed the first group of admonitions within a framework alluding to love, so this second one is enclosed by the admonition: "Welcome one another!" (15:7-12. Cf. 14:1). At this point Paul concludes the letter with a wish, invoking peace (15:13). The initial part of the wish is 15:5 f.

F. A POSTSCRIPT (Romans 15:14-33)

1. A justification of the letter (15:14-21)
2. An announcement and explanation concerning his coming (15:22-29)
3. Paul requests the intercession of the congregation at Rome (15:30-32)
4. Benediction of peace (15:33)

In this postscript Paul explains the significance of his Letter to the Romans (15:14-21). He announces that he is going to Rome, mentions what relevance this trip will have (15:22-29), and asks for the intercession of the congregation (15:30-32). The postscript is concluded with another invocation of peace (15:33).

Chapter 16 is an addition to Romans. (It is uncertain whether it is for the church at Rome or another congregation—perhaps the church at Ephesus.)* It includes a commendation to the church deaconess Phoebe (vv. 1-2), a long list of mutual greetings (vv. 3-16, 21-23), as well as a warning against false teachers (vv. 17-20), and a benediction (vv. 25-27).

---

*Translator's Note: The large number of salutations in this chapter (vv. 3-16, 21-23) suggest that Paul knew a large number of Christians in the place to which he was writing. This would be surprising for the church at Rome, since he had as yet not visited it. It is therefore quite possible that these greetings refer to people in Ephesus, where he had worked more than two years. The denunciatory tone of part of the chapter also suggests that Paul was writing to a community that knew him and acknowledged his authority.

VIII

The First Letter to the Corinthians

Paul wrote this letter in Ephesus in the year 53 to the congregation he had established in Corinth. In it he answers a letter written to him by the Corinthians (mentioned in 1 Cor. 7:1). This in turn had been a response to an initial letter by Paul, which unfortunately is not extant. In this present letter we are able to share something of the growth of the first missionary congregations, who were left on their own, after the apostle had been with them but a short time. This explains the deep significance of this congregational letter.

It was unavoidable that problems should arise in a church left to itself in this way. In Corinth there was a growing division, especially between those who thought of themselves as possessing a deeper spiritual understanding and the many others who in comparison were looked upon as simple lay folk. There were additional factions as well that had been formed.

Paul answers in this epistle a series of questions, addressed to him in the letter from the Corinthians. The arrangement of the epistle has been determined from this standpoint. The many topics, listed by Paul one after the other without any definite order, may be arranged roughly in the following groups:

1. Factions in the congregation (1:1—4:21)
2. Moral abuses in the congregation (5:1—6:20)
3. The congregation in the world (7:1—11:1)
4. The public worship of the congregation (11:2—14:40)
5. Concerning the resurrection of the dead (15:1-58)
6. The conclusion of the letter (16:1-24)

91

The epistle may be represented in chart form as follows:

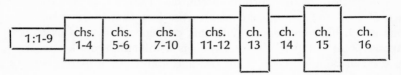

| 1:1-9 | chs. 1-4 | chs. 5-6 | chs. 7-10 | chs. 11-12 | ch. 13 | ch. 14 | ch. 15 | ch. 16 |

A. THE SALUTATION (1 Cor. 1:1-9)

After an indication of the sender of the letter, the place to which it was addressed, and a greeting (1:1-2), comes the apostle's expression of gratitude for the grace that had been granted to the congregation in a rich variety of divine gifts. Through this abundance they would be preserved by God's faithfulness until the day of Christ's return.

B. FACTIONS IN THE CONGREGATION (1 Cor. 1:10—4:21)

1. An appeal for unity in opposition to the formation of factions (1:10-17)

2. The power of God in the message of the cross (1:18-25)
   a. As indicated by the church in Corinth (1:26-31)
   b. As indicated by Paul's appearance in Corinth (2:1-5)
      The wisdom of God (2:6-16)
   c. As indicated by the factions in Corinth (3:1-4; cf. 1:12)

3. The foundation and structure of the congregation (3:5-23)
   a. The apostles are but servants of Christ (4:1-8)
   b. The sufferings and disgrace of the servants of Christ (4:9-13)

4. The conclusion of the admonition (4:14-21)

This first part of the letter starts off with an admonition to unity and closes again in the same way. The basis for this admonition proceeds along two lines of thought:

(a) The word of the cross is power (1:18, 24).* The wisdom of God, revealed in this word of the cross, is a wisdom that is concealed in the preaching of the crucified Christ under the guise of

---

*At the beginning of Romans the theme likewise concerns the power of God (1:16).

foolishness and scandal (1:18-25). This hiddenness is indicated in the composition of the Corinthian church (1:26-31), in the appearance of Paul in Corinth, and also in the fact that there were factions which had developed. With this reference Paul returns to his starting point (1:10-17). In between is a difficult remark concerning the wisdom of God. This passage stands in a parenthetical position in 2:6-16.

(b) Along a second line Paul establishes the hiddenness of wisdom within the preaching of the cross. This he does from the standpoint of the apostolic office. There is a false idea of the apostolic office he suggests that is inherent in the factions that are calling themselves after Paul and Apollos. The apostles are nothing but servants, each with his particular assignment. It is only the foundation that is decisive for the church and its structure: "For no other foundation can anyone lay than that which is laid, which is Jesus Christ . . . " (3:5-23).

The apostles are ministers of Christ and stewards in charge of the mysteries of God. With them everything depends upon the faithfulness with which they serve (4:1-8). This faithfulness must be confirmed in suffering and disgrace. If the hiddenness of the preaching of the cross is manifest anywhere, it is here. "God has exhibited us apostles as last of all," Paul says (4:9). After this subtle rebuke against the spiritual presumptuousness of the Corinthians, Paul repeats his admonition to the congregation (4:14-21).

C. MORAL ABUSES IN THE CONGREGATION (1 Cor. 5—6)

Spiritual arrogance had given rise to moral abuses in the congregation. Paul cites some examples of which he had heard: a case of incest (5:1-5) that gave him the occasion to warn against association with members of the congregation who were immoral (5:6-13), the arbitration of cases involving members of the congregation before heathen law courts (6:1-11), sins of immorality (6:12-20). In connection with each of these abuses Paul shows the congregation the honor and dignity of being a Christian: "Do you not know that your body is a temple of the Holy Spirit?"

D. THE CONGREGATION IN THE WORLD
(1 Cor. 7:1—11:1)

1. Concerning marriage and celibacy (7:1-40)

    a. The advantage of celibacy, the concession of marriage (7:1-9)
    b. The command of the Lord in regard to divorce (7:10-11)
    c. Advice in relation to marriage between Christians and pagans (7:12-17)
    d. "Everyone should remain in the state in which he was called" (7:18-24)
    e. Advice for the unmarried (7:25-38)
    f. Advice for widows (7:39-40)

2. Concerning the eating of meat offered to idols (8:1—11:1)

    a. For us there is but one God (8:1-6)
    b. Nevertheless have consideration for the weak (8:7-13)
    c. Paul had given up his right of maintenance (9:1-18)
    d. He has made himself a slave to all (9:19-23)
    e. The athlete (9:24-27)
    f. The Israelites in the wilderness (10:1-13)
    g. "The table of the Lord or the table of demons" (10:14-22)
    h. Admonition: Do not give offense! (10:23—11:1)

What Paul says here about marriage is mentioned in expectation of the Lord's imminent return. From this point of view he gives celibacy the priority and concedes the value of marriage in order to preserve one from licentiousness (7:1-9). Here as elsewhere Paul advises Christians to remain in the state in which they have been called (7:18-24). This applies also to marriages between Christians and pagans (7:12-17). The instructions that Paul then gives on behalf of the unmarried (7:25-38) and widows (7:39-40) all have the same intent: "I want you to be free from anxieties!" (7:32-36, cf. v. 28). Therefore the statement, "having as though we did not have," also applies to marriage. Paul's concern in this chapter is not with marriage as an order of life, but with the Christian's "undivided devotion to the Lord," because (as he says) the "time is short."

The questions about meat offered to idols have to do essentially with the issue of the Christians' participation in the social life of their time. Fundamentally Paul was on the side of those for whom this question had lost its meaning, because as he says, "we know that there is no God but one!" (8:1-6). But this realization was not the same among all. Therefore one should have consideration for the weak. Correct understanding is vitiated, when the one point of view is set above the others, so that it becomes a stumbling-block for the others (8:7-13; 10:23—11:1).

Paul again as in chs. 1—4 alludes to an example from his own experience. He would have the right to claim support for his ministry to the churches but he had relinquished this privilege (9:1-18). What is more, he had made himself a servant to all for the sake of the gospel. For the weak he had become weak in order to win them for Christ (9:19-23). He had been able to renounce anything when it had to do with the imperishable wreath (9:24-27).

He likens the progress of the church to the progress of the ancient people of God in the wilderness (10:1-13), comparing the trials at that time with the ones of the present. "Any one who thinks that he stands," he says, "take heed lest he fall!" (10:1-13). Paragraph 10:14-22 leads already over to the larger section (11:2—14:40).

E. THE WORSHIP OF THE CONGREGATION
(1 Cor. 11:2—14:40)

1. The covering of a woman's head at public worship (11:2-16)

2. An unworthy celebration of the Lord's Supper (11:17-34)

3. Spiritual gifts (12:1—14:46)
   a. Varieties of gifts but one Spirit (12:1-11)
   b. Many members but one body (12:12-31)
   c. The hymn of love (13:1-13)
   d. Intelligible speech and speaking in tongues (14:1-25)
   e. "All things should be done . . . in order!" (14:26-40)

Paul's observations here concerning primitive Christian worship are almost completely removed from our form of worship service.

It is particularly important therefore to take special note of the essential points. Paul speaks of the modes of worship (11:2-16; 14:26-40), the public celebration of the Lord's Supper (11:17-34), and the word at divine service (12:1—14:40).

At the heart of the whole section is Paul's hymn on love, which is really his decisive word concerning the public worship of a Christian congregation. In its position at the center of chs. 12—14 the hymn establishes the superiority of intelligible utterance (i.e., speech that edifies the church) over ecstatic speaking in tongues. The latter was looked upon as the most outstanding of spiritual gifts. "He who speaks in tongues edifies himself," Paul says (14:4). We would probably say that speaking in tongues is an expression of religious individualism. But this is really not the purpose of a Christian worship service. It is rather for the "upbuilding" of the church as the body of Christ, in which all are members. This occurs, however, in preaching, in intelligible language that is able to comfort and admonish—not only those who already are Christians but also those who are not (14:23-25). It is actually and essentially God's love, given and revealed to the world in Christ, which is the concern of worship in a Christian congregation.

In contrast to the extravagant religiosity exhibited when one speaks in tongues, Paul praises the exuberance of love in which God has come to men (cf. John 3:16; Ps. 113), the love which in the worship of the church is to be passed on to mankind, for whom it is intended. This occurs, however, when there is preaching, prayer, and praise in sensible, intelligible words.

It is only in this love that the Lord's Supper can be worthily celebrated (11:17-34). What Paul had received from the Lord in the words of institution and has transmitted to the church in Corinth (11:23-26) is abused when "one is hungry and another is drunk." When Paul concludes his instructions for celebrating the Lord's Supper with the sober admonition: "When you come together to eat, wait for one another!" he is pointing to love as the basic attitude that is also essential for the Lord's Supper.

This love extends even into the visible forms of worship (11:2-16; 14:26-40). Paul alludes to the veiling of women as an example of the fact that the Spirit's presence does not simply abolish what is natural and customary. Unbounded love, which "does not insist on its own way," extends even to the observance of custom and order.

What Paul in this section actually wants to say concerning church worship is found not so much in the individual instructions. It is rather in the passionate allusion to God's love revealed in Christ. This is the vital heart of Christian worship.

F. THE HOPE OF THE CHURCH (1 Cor. 15)

1. The message of the resurrection (15:1-11)
2. The dispute in Corinth over the resurrection (15:12-19)
3. The foundation for and the event of the resurrection (15:20-28)
4. The consequences of their dispute (15:29-34)
5. How are the dead raised? (15:35-49)
6. The perishable shall put on the imperishable (15:50-53)
7. The rejoicing of the redeemed (15:54-58)

This great concluding chapter concerning the hope of the church is most clearly revealed in its final words (cf. Rom. 8:31 ff.; 11:33 ff.). What Paul is actually setting up over against those in Corinth who were denying the resurrection is the joyful, unconditional assurance concerning Christ's victory over sin and death: "But thanks be to God who gives us the victory through our Lord Jesus Christ!" This assurance is founded on the message of Christ's resurrection (15:1-11), which Paul had received and transmitted to the Corinthians (cf. 11:23). With this certainty everything stands or falls (so says Paul). Wherever the resurrection of the dead is disputed, there also the resurrection of Christ is denied, and then the faith becomes absolutely futile. "If in this life we who are in Christ have only *hope*, we are of all men most to be pitied" (15:19). Directly related to this statement is the final sentence in ch. 15: "Therefore, my beloved brethren, be steadfast, immovable, always abounding in the work of the Lord, knowing that in the Lord your labor is not in vain."

The explanatory paragraphs from vv. 20-53 are to be associated with and subordinated to this unquestioning thankful assurance concerning the resurrection, upon which the message of Christ's resurrection rests. The paragraphs can only make reference to the miracle of the resurrection; they are unable to make it understandable. The resurrection is based on Christ's work (15:20-22), that initiates a new human epoch. The ultimate goal of his work is the destruction of death (15:23-28), "so that God may be all in all."

To the question as to how the dead are raised (15:35-49) Paul can only respond with metaphors. This question does not permit a direct answer, because "what is sown is perishable, what is raised is imperishable" (15:42, 50-53). The message of the resurrection, which Paul develops in this chapter and by which faith in Christ stands or falls can be perceived correctly only against the background of the Old Testament. It is to be noted especially in the praise of those rescued from the power of death as expressed in the psalms of thanksgiving* or in the assurance of one who has been exposed to death (Ps. 73; Job 19); it is to be discerned in the songs of the Suffering Servant, whose vicarious death is endorsed by God (Isa. 53).†

Just as the Old Testament reaches a summit in the message concerning the resurrection of the people of God (Ezek. 37), so the New Testament comes to a climax in its message concerning victory over death in the resurrection of Christ (1 Cor. 15:1-11, 54-58).

G. THE CONCLUSION OF THE LETTER (1 Cor. 16)

1. The collections for Jerusalem (16:1-4)
2. An announcement of Paul's visit to Corinth, Timothy and Apollos (16:5-12)
3. A final admonition (16:13-18)
4. Greetings and a personally-written conclusion (16:19-24)

---

*Translator's Note: Cf. Westermann, *Handbook to the Old Testament*, pp. 219 f.

†*Ibid.*, p. 150.

IX

The Second Letter to the Corinthians

Second Corinthians reflects in a most agitated manner the struggles of Paul for his congregation in Corinth. The details of the controversy and ultimate reconciliation are bewildering to the modern day reader. What really went on between Paul and the congregation cannot be determined from the drift of the letter as we now have it. It is necessary first of all to describe the letter itself and then make an attempt to set in order the events that are implied in between the lines.

The tone of the whole letter is set by Paul's affirmation and defense of his office as an apostle. The authority lying behind this office had been challenged by his opponents in Corinth. It was necessary for Paul therefore to intercede on behalf of the message he had to bring. He does so by defending his office and his work, frequently mentioning that he has been forced to intercede for his message in this round-about way simply because of his opponents in Corinth.

In chs. 1—7 he upholds the significance and duty of his apostolic office. In this connection the note of joyous gratitude predominates in chs. 1—2 and 7. Chs. 8 and 9 deal only with the offering for Jerusalem; chs. 10-13 represent a sharp and impassioned argument with the congregation, which here seems to be on the point of disowning Paul entirely.

A. PAUL'S APOSTOLIC OFFICE (2 Cor. 1—7)

1. Salutation (1:1-2)
2. Praise of the God of all comfort (Rescue from deadly peril) (1:3-11)

99

3. The apostle's boast (You are my pride, I am yours) (1:12-14)
4. Why Paul did not come to Corinth (1:15—2:4)
5. Concluding comment concerning the punishment of the offender (2:5-11)
6. The fond expectation of seeing Titus in Troas (2:12-13)
7. Paul's service—a fragrance to life and to death (2:14-17)
8. "You are our letter of introduction" (3:1-3)
9. "Ministers of a new covenant" (3:4-11)
10. The veil is removed (3:12-18)
11. We preach "the gospel of the glory of Christ" (4:1-6)
12. Carrying in the body thereby his death (4:7-12)
13. In the assurance of his glory (4:13-18)
14. We are certain of a home with the Lord (5:1-10)
15. Ambassadors for Christ in the ministry of reconciliation (5:11-21)
16. Final admonition: Receive me! (6:1-13; 7:2-4)
    The servant of God in many afflictions (vv. 3-10)
17. A warning against fellowship with unbelievers (6:14—7:1)

B. JOY OVER THE GOOD NEWS BROUGHT BY TITUS IN TROAS (2 Cor. 7:5-7, 13-16)

The godly grief produced by the sorrowful letter (7:8-13).

C. THE COLLECTION FOR JERUSALEM (2 Cor. 8—9)

D. PAUL'S STRUGGLE FOR HIS CONGREGATION (2 Cor. 10—13)

1. Paul has to defend himself against the charge that he is acting in a worldly fashion (10:1-6)
2. He can only boast of what Christ has done through him (10:7-18)
3. The "superlative apostles" are false apostles (11:1-15)
   Why Paul worked without compensation (vv. 7-12)
4. Words spoken in foolishness (11:16—12:18)
   a. Paul's boast (11:16-22)
   b. Paul's suffering in Christ's service (11:23-33)
   c. A secret revelation (12:1-6)
   d. The thorn in the flesh and suffering for the sake of Christ (12:7-10)
   e. Paul is not inferior to the "superlative apostles" (12:11-18)
      Paul's working without compensation (vv. 4-18)
5. Paul announces that his third coming will be drastic and unsparing (12:19—13:10)
6. Closing admonition and wish (13:11-13)

Even a mere survey sets forth clearly three sections (other than the chapters dealing with the collection). These are concerned with:

(1) Paul's reconciliation with the congregation (1:1—2:13; 7:5-16)

(2) His apostolic ministry (2:14—6:13)

(3) His struggle for his congregation (10:1—13:10)

The first two sections are interwoven with each other. This can be easily perceived in the way 7:5 ff. fits in closely with 2:12-13. In between has been inserted chs. 2:14—7:4, which is complete in itself. It ends in the final admonition (6:1-13; 7:2-4).

A special difficulty is presented by chs. 10—13, in which the tone of Paul is so caustic and bitter. This attitude is hardly comprehensible in the same letter that begins in chs. 2—4 with such grateful joy because of the reconciliation with the Corinthian church. To solve this difficulty (and others as well), G. Bornkamm* has suggested that one should consider 2 Cor. to be a later combination of several Pauline letters or parts of letters, destined to be passed on to other churches. Taken in sequence, they can better account for the reactions between Paul and the Corinthian church.

The section that was written earliest in time according to this view would be chs. 2:14—7:4, which describe Paul's apostolic ministry. After this letter Paul visited the congregation and found them in complete defection from him. In concern and sorrow over his congregation he then wrote the "tearful letter" (chs. 10—13). (It has been long assumed that these chapters represent in whole or in part the letter that Paul mentions in 7:8-13 as having been written in tears.) This letter and the subsequent visit of Titus (2:12 f.) effected a change, and this is attested in grateful joy by the "letter of reconciliation" (1:1—2:13; 7:5-16). These letters or portions of letters were then later combined in the Corinthian church itself into a Pauline letter, a letter that was destined to be passed on to other churches.

---

*G. Bornkamm, "The History of the origin of the so-called Second Letter to the Corinthians," *New Testament Studies,* Vol. 8, pp. 258-264.

The following chart indicates the arrangement of these letters:

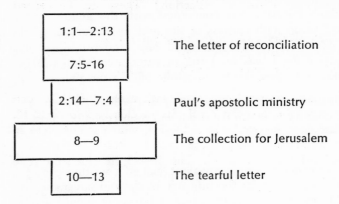

1:1—2:13	The letter of reconciliation
7:5-16	
2:14—7:4	Paul's apostolic ministry
8—9	The collection for Jerusalem
10—13	The tearful letter

A. THE LETTER OF RECONCILIATION
(2 Cor. 1:1—2:13)

After the introductory greeting Paul informs the congregation that he had been rescued from a deadly peril while traveling in Asia Minor. He also associates this event with his ministry to the church, indicating that he had been comforted in order that he might share this comfort with others (1:3-11). Even his boast that he had performed his service by God's grace was not intended by him for his own benefit. "You can be proud of us," he says, "as we can be proud of you" (1:12-14).

He had failed to come to Corinth as announced only in order to spare them. Therefore he had written the letter "with many tears" (1:15–2:4). Now that the man whose conduct had shocked Paul had been punished, the congregation may forgive him, even as had Paul (2:5-11). Paul had desired so earnestly to get a report from Corinth that he had traveled on to find Titus (2:12-13). When he had met him then in Macedonia, he had derived joy and comfort from the news that Titus had brought out of Corinth (7:5-7; 13-16). Thus the tearful letter, even though it had brought sorrow at first, did produce repentance and through repentance fruit for that which was good.

B. PAUL'S APOSTOLIC MINISTRY (2 Cor. 2:14—7:4)

Because Paul's ministry was concerned with the genuine word
of God, it had to do with matters of life and death for those who
heard it (2:14-17). Paul did not need any credentials for this.
The congregation itself was his letter of recommendation (3:1-3).
Paul then goes on to describe his apostolic office from two aspects:

(1) It is the ministry of a new covenant in the freedom of the Spirit.
(2) It is a ministry in which the death and resurrection of Christ are
embodied.

(1)

Paul is the minister of a new covenant "not in a written code but
in the Spirit" (3:6). If even the ministry of the old covenant (the
ministry of Moses) had glory, then how much more should not the
new covenant have! (3:4-11). The veil that Moses had is taken
away for those who believe in Christ. "Where the Spirit of the
Lord is, there is freedom" (3:12-18).

(2)

The shining of the glory of God in Christ is continuing on in
Paul's ministry (4:1-6). In the outward form of this ministry Paul
bears in himself the suffering and death of Christ (4:7-12). In the
assurance of the resurrection, however, every affliction is "preparing . . . an eternal weight of glory beyond all comparison"
(4:13-18). For (as Paul says) we are certain of the eternal home
(5:1-10). Jesus' death and resurrection thus become effective in
the ministry of the one who is an ambassador for Christ. It is a
ministry of reconciliation (5:11-21).

In a final admonition Paul requests the Corinthians to receive
him, even as his heart had been opened wide to them (6:1-13;
7:2-4). They were indeed the ones in whose fellowship he had
found comfort and joy in his severe afflictions. "As dying and behold we live . . . " (In this paragraph is a deeply moving list of
contrasting clauses—6:3-10).

His warning against fellowship with unbelievers was probably
added later (6:14—7:1).

C. THE COLLECTION FOR JERUSALEM (2 Cor. 8—9)

The Macedonian churches had contributed gladly and freely (8:1-6). "Prove now your love," Paul says, "by eager readiness to give" (8:7-15). The delivery of the donation lay in good hands (8:16-24). Paul was sending messengers in advance to make ready for the offerings (9:1-5). At the close is an admonition to give cheerfully in praise of God (9:6-15).

D. THE TEARFUL LETTER. THE STRUGGLE OF PAUL FOR HIS CONGREGATION (2 Cor. 10—13)

Paul turns deliberately against the people in Corinth who are reproaching him for reprehensible conduct. In obedience to Christ he must strive much more against thoughts that are an obstacle to the knowledge of God (10:1-6). They were saying of him: "It is merely in his letters that he is powerful. His personal appearance, however, is weak." To this Paul counters that he does not intend to boast beyond limit as do his opponents. Instead he refers to that which lay before their eyes—his missionary work, which Christ had accomplished through him (10:7-18).

He was not inferior in any way to the "superlative apostles" in Corinth. On the contrary, where they were preaching another Christ and mediating another spirit than Paul, they were deceivers and false apostles (11:1-15).

At the same time, Paul had to defend himself even against a malicious interpretation of his refusal to accept compensation from the Corinthian church. It had been his purpose simply not to be in any way a burden to the congregation (11:7-12; 12:14-18).

Included within these two paragraphs is Paul's response to his opponents who had been bragging about themselves as over against him. He responds in self-glorification that is admittedly foolish. But it then turns out to be simply a boast in his own weakness (11:16—12:13). Paul would have been able to boast of what he was (11:21-23a). He intended, however, to boast only of his suffering in the service of Christ (11:23b-33). He would have been able to boast of sublime revelations (12:1-6). He intended rather to boast only of his "thorn in the flesh" (12:7-10), from which the Lord had not liberated him despite his pleading. It was in *this* sense that Paul wanted his claim to be understood that he was not inferior to the "superlative apostles."

The conclusion of the letter (12:19–13:13): Considering the present situation Paul was afraid that he would come across unpleasant conditions in Corinth (12:19-21). In the event of this he declares that he will act unsparingly, when he comes to Corinth (13:1-4). He hopes, however, that it will not come to this. He has his authority indeed not to tear down but to build up (13:5-10). As a conclusion he admonishes the congregation to live in peace, declaring: "And the God of love and peace will be with you" (13:11-13).

X

The Letter to the Galatians

Paul wrote his letter to the Galatians from Ephesus in the year 53. It was a circular letter, addressed to several congregations that Paul had established in the region of Galatia* (Acts 16:8). He saw that these churches were being threatened by a Judeo-Christian doctrine, in which apparently the law and circumcision were considered as an additional requirement for salvation. Christ and his baptism seem to have been understood as a fulfillment of the religion of the law, linking the Christian with an order that affected world destiny. The proclamation of the gospel as the end of the law and the apostolic claim of Paul were being flatly rejected.

It is in the light of this situation that Paul's caustic tone in addressing his congregation is to be understood. It was not simply a matter of another dogma but the question of abiding with Christ.

In chs. 1–4 Paul explains the origin and nature of the gospel that he had preached to the Galatians. In chs. 5–6 he discusses the realization of freedom, for which this gospel brings liberation.

1:1-5	Salutation (1:1-5)
1:6-12	The Gospel preached by Paul (1:6-12)
1:13—2:21	Not of human origin (1:13—2:21)
3:1—4:31	Not of human character (3:1—4:31)
5:1—6:10	The realization of freedom (5:1—6:10)
6:11-18	Autographic postscript (6:11-18)

---

*Translator's Note: In Paul's day the term Galatia, derived from an ethnic group called Galatians living near Ancyra (modern Ankara), was applied to a large Roman province in eastern Asia Minor. (See map inside back cover.) It included the southern cities of Derbe, Lystra, Iconium, and Pisidian Antioch.

A. THE GOSPEL PREACHED BY PAUL (Gal. 1:1-12)

1. Salutation, greeting of peace (1:1-5)
2. A curse on the one who preaches another gospel (1:6-10)
3. The true gospel is not of human character or origin (1:11-12)

B. IT IS NOT OF HUMAN ORIGIN (Gal. 1:13—2:21)

1. How Paul became a messenger of the gospel (1:13-24)
2. Paul was acknowledged as an apostle to the Gentiles by the "pillars" in Jerusalem (2:1-10)
3. Paul had defended the free gospel even against Peter (2:11-21)

The curse with which the letter begins (1:6-10), pronounced on those who were corrupting the gospel, indicates with what grave earnestness Paul was struggling here to hold on to his congregation. Paul, who himself had previously persecuted the Christians, had received the message he was proclaiming to the Galatians directly from Christ (1:13-24). That he was really doing the work of Jesus Christ among the Gentiles had been recognized by the apostles in Jerusalem. They themselves had confirmed Paul in his apostleship to the Gentiles without placing any kind of restrictions upon him (2:1-10). Paul indeed had openly stood up for the freedom of the gospel in the face of Peter's inconsistency. He had done this "in order to be justified by faith in Christ and not by works of the law" (2:16). If justification had come by works, then Christ would have died in vain (2:11-21).

C. IT IS NOT OF A HUMAN CHARACTER (Gal. 3—4)

1. An appeal to the Galatians' own experience (3:1-5)
2. Abraham: curse and blessing separate in respect to faith (3:6-14)
3. Abraham's inheritance according to promise (3:15-29)
4. We are all heirs as those who were redeemed (4:1-7)
5. An appeal to the experience of the Galatians (4:8-20)
6. Children of the slave and children of the free woman (4:21-31)

This section begins and ends with an appeal to the Galatians. Paul reminds them of how "Jesus Christ was publicly portrayed before their eyes as crucified." He asks them: "Did you experience

---

These were visited by Paul on his First Missionary Journey (Acts 13 f.). According to a South Galatian theory, favored by many scholars, these were the churches to whom Paul wrote this letter. Other scholars favor a North Galatian theory and limit the term "Galatians" to the ethnic group bearing that name.

so many things in vain?" (3:1-5). He reminds them of how they
then had received him even though he had preached to them
because of a bodily ailment, and they would have done anything
for him (4:8-20).

The gospel that he proclaims has to do with a fundamental
line of demarcation. Those who with Abraham have faith (cf.
Rom. 4) belong on the side of blessing; those who are under the
law belong on the side of a curse (3:6-14). Those who have become
sons through faith are no longer slaves but heirs (3:26—4:7). But
with this (he says) it follows that the other line of demarcation
in regard to what you formerly have been is removed: "For you
are all one in Christ Jesus" (3:28).

The appended scriptural proof in 4:21-31, is unusual, as to
the way the Old Testament is interpreted. It adds nothing that
is essentially different from what has already been said.

D. THE REALIZATION OF FREEDOM (Gal. 5—6)

1. Christ has freed us for love (5:1-6)
2. A repeated appeal to the congregation (5:7-12)
3. Freedom for love (5:13-15)
4. The works of the flesh and the fruit of the Spirit (5:16-26)
5. "Bear one another's burdens" (6:1-5)
6. "Whatever a man sows that he will also reap" (6:6-10)
7. Autographic postscript (6:11-18)

Paul's concern in this letter is condensed into a few sentences
in 5:1-6: There is only an "either-or." To accept the law as a means
of salvation means to sever oneself from Christ. Faith in Christ,
however, exists in order to prove itself effective in love.

"You were called to freedom," Paul tells the Galatians. But this
freedom lies only in a serious acceptance of the law of love
(5:13-15). In contrasting the works of the flesh and the fruit of the
Spirit (5:16-26), Paul begins the listing of the latter with: "The
fruit of the Spirit is love . . . "

When Paul sounds an urgent warning against the false teachers
in his autographic conclusion, he is professing in this way his love
for the Galatian church, whom he commends at the end to the
grace of the Lord.

XI

The Letter to the Ephesians

In especially solemn language that at times has a liturgical character this letter deals with the wonder and mystery of the Christian church, which embraces Jews and Gentiles and extends into cosmic dimensions. The first part of the letter is written from the standpoint of praise (chs. 1–3); the second from that of exhortation (chs. 4–6). There is little to be perceived, however, in regard to the concrete circumstances of the congregation, concerning the apostle's personal relationship with it, concerning joy or anguish as a mutual concern. There is much that is different from other Pauline letters in the language, the ideas, the theological concepts. Much, however, is quite distinctly reminiscent of these letters.

Many exegetes have accordingly assumed that the letter was written in the spirit of Paul by one of his students and for this reason attributed to him. (This was at that time an appropriate way of appealing to the authority of the person in question. One should by no means use such language as authentic or spurious in this connection.)

The epistle may be represented in chart form as follows:

1:1-23	Salutation, thanksgiving, and intercession (1:1-23)
2:1-10	He has made those who were dead alive (2:1-10)
2:11-22	He has brought near those who were far off (2:11-22)
3:1-13	He has caused the mystery to be proclaimed through Paul's apostleship (3:1-13)
3:14-21	Intercession and praise (3:14-21)
4:1—6:23	Exhortation (4:1—6:23)

A. PRAISE, THANKSGIVING AND INTERCESSION
(Eph. 1—3)

1. Salutation (1:1-2)

2. Thanksgiving (1:3-14)

3. Intercession (1:15-23)

> He has made alive those who were dead (2:1-10)
> He has brought near those who were far-off (2:11-22)
> He has caused the mystery to be proclaimed through Paul's apostleship (3:1-13)

4. Intercession and praise (3:14-21)

After the introductory greeting the letter opens with a tribute to God, who is praised for his redemptive work on our behalf through Christ. By it we may become something significant to the praise of his glory (1:3-14). The apostle directs his petition also to the end that the church may know the exceeding rich and profound mystery of her calling. This calling has made her a participant in Christ's work, that embraces heaven and earth (1:15-23). This work of Christ is then explained in 2:1—3:13.

(a) Those who through their sins were under the dominion of death have become heirs of the work of redemption. They have been restored to life and exalted with Christ (2:1-10).

(b) Christ has broken down the dividing wall between Jews and Gentiles so as to make into one new man the two factions that were distant toward each other. Both are growing into a new structure, built upon the foundation of the apostles and the prophets (2:11-22).

The mystery of this work of redemption has been revealed to the "holy apostles and prophets." They are supposed to make it known to the Gentiles as good news, and the heavenly powers have a share in it (3:1-13).

After this exhibition of Christ's work of salvation, the apostle once more offers up prayers, intercessions, and praise (3:20-21). The intercessory prayers correspond to those of 1:15-23, and his final words terminate again in praise of God's glory (as in 1:3-14).

B. EXHORTATION (Parenesis) (Eph. 4—6)

1. An admonition to unity (4:1-6)
2. Christ has granted spiritual gifts to his church (4:7-13)
3. Through these gifts the members are supposed to grow up to him who is the head (4:14-16)
4. "Put on the new nature!" (4:17-24)
5. Admonitions for daily living (4:25-32)
6. Separation from darkness, walking in the light (5:1-21)
7. A table of duties for the Christian household (5:21—6:9)
8. The Christian armor (6:10-17)
9. An admonition to intercession (6:18-20)
10. Conclusion to the letter (6:21-24)

The admonition to maintain unity, with which the hortatory section begins, corresponds to that which had been said before about the church. Here is one of the most powerful and lucid observations of the New Testament regarding the unity of the church (4:4-6): "One Lord—one faith—one baptism . . . "

Contributing to this unity is the diversity of the gifts that Christ acquired for his church by means of his way of redemption into the heights and into the depths (4:7-13). These gifts were also intended to serve for building the body of Christ. The imagery of the body (4:14-16) corresponds here to that of the temple in 2:20 f.

Out of this imagery issues the admonition for the individual Christian not to live as the Gentiles but to put on the new nature (4:17-24). Concrete examples of this are then given in many separate admonitions (4:25-32).

Every pagan conduct belongs to darkness. Christians, however, are to be children of light (5:1-21). At this point an early Christian baptismal hymn has probably been cited:

> "Awake, O sleeper, and arise from the dead,
> and Christ shall give you light" (5:14).

The admonitions on behalf of social ranks in the congregation are formulated in a table of household duties, as was also in vogue at that time (5:21—6:9). In this table Christ's relationship to the church is compared with marriage.

The broadly amplified illustration of a Christian's being armed for battle against the principalities and powers (6:10-17) forms the conclusion of the hortatory section.

The letter closes with a request for intercessory prayer, an announcement concerning Tychicus, and a greeting of peace (6:18-24).

XII

The Letter to the Philippians

The letter was probably written by Paul in Ephesus during his imprisonment there (2 Cor. 1:8).* Philippi was the first congregation that Paul founded on European soil in the year 49/50 (Acts 16:11-40).

The occasion for the letter was an offering that the congregation had forwarded to him by means of Epaphroditus (2:25-30), who had become severely ill during his stay with Paul. Paul had then sent him back with the letter. The relationship of Paul to this congregation was an especially friendly one. Extending throughout the letter is the summons to rejoice.

Paul desired to thank the church at Philippi for the gift that they had sent over to him by Epaphroditus. This expression of gratitude, however, does not come until the end of the letter (4:10-20). Paul begins by giving a report concerning his lot in prison. Nevertheless, this account directs one away from Paul to Christ, and so at the heart of the letter is the hymn concerning Christ (2:5-11).

---

*Translator's Note: Because of the reference to the praetorian guard (1:12) and Caesar's household (4:22) the letter has been commonly considered to have been written during Paul's imprisonment in Rome (ca. 61-63). The indications, however, are by no means conclusive. An inscription from Ephesus (J. T. Wood, *Discoveries at Ephesus,* 1877) indicates that praetorian soldiers were stationed there. Another inscription speaks of "the slaves of our Lord Augustus," in other words, "members of Caesar's household." Paul's expectation to visit Philippi soon (2:24) would be quite natural, if the letter had been written from Ephesus. There is, of course, no mention in Acts of any imprisonment in Ephesus. Paul's reference in 1 Cor. 15:32, to "fighting with wild beasts in Ephesus" has been thought by some to imply physical hardship, leading to imprisonment. Cf. also 2 Cor. 1:8.

An outline of Philippians in the form of a chart is as follows:

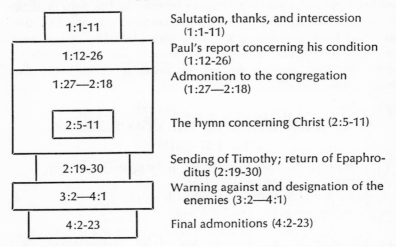

1:1-11	Salutation, thanks, and intercession (1:1-11)
1:12-26	Paul's report concerning his condition (1:12-26)
1:27—2:18	Admonition to the congregation (1:27—2:18)
2:5-11	The hymn concerning Christ (2:5-11)
2:19-30	Sending of Timothy; return of Epaphroditus (2:19-30)
3:2—4:1	Warning against and designation of the enemies (3:2—4:1)
4:2-23	Final admonitions (4:2-23)

A. SALUTATION, THANKSGIVING, AND INTERCESSION
(Phil. 1—3)

1. Salutation (1:1-2)
2. Thanksgiving and intercession for the church in Philippi (1:3-11)

Paul's gratitude and intercession (1:3-11) sound the keynote of this letter: "In every prayer of mine for you all making my prayer with joy" (v. 4). Paul thinks of the Philippians in happy assurance—God will complete the good work that he has begun in them.

B. PAUL'S REPORT CONCERNING HIS CONDITION
(Phil. 1:12-26)

1. His imprisonment has served to advance the gospel (1:12-18)
2. Christ will be glorified through him, whether by life or death (1:19-26; 2:17 f.)

In the account of his plight Paul in the initial sentence turns away from the harsh facts of his imprisonment to the results God had accomplished thereby. The message had gained wider circulation precisely through this experience, and although there may also have been present some very human motives in the case of those who brought the message, what really mattered was the fact that Christ had been proclaimed in every way (1:12-18). When Paul peers into the future, however, he knows that Christ will be glorified by him, whether through his death or through his continuing to live (1:19-26).

C. AN ADMONITION TO THE CONGREGATION
(Phil. 1:27—2:18)

1. "Let your manner of life be worthy of the gospel!" (1:27-30)
2. "Being . . . of one mind" (2:1-5)
3. As our Lord (the hymn concerning Christ) (2:5-11)
4. Walk worthily of this Lord! (2:12-16)

As soon as he has given an account of his circumstances, Paul proceeds to his admonishment of the Philippians. But his admonition to lead a life that is worthy of the gospel and of the Lord leads to the real heart of the letter. This is the hymn concerning Christ (2:5-11). It is introduced with the words: "Have this mind among yourselves, which you have in Christ Jesus" (2:5). It was already one of the oldest hymns concerning Christ's humility and exaltation and the ultimate goal thereof. It derived its distinctive style perhaps in the worship service of the earliest Christian congregations. In 2:12-16 the admonition is once more adopted and closely associated with an account of Paul's condition, so that the admonition can conclude with the summons: "Rejoice with me."

D. THE ANNOUNCEMENT CONCERNING TIMOTHY AND THE RETURN OF EPAPHRODITUS (Phil. 2:19-30)

The fundamental note of joy is present also in these simple communications. There was nothing too trivial for Paul in his association with his congregation but what it had some connection with the progress of the gospel.

E. THE WARNING AGAINST THE ENEMIES
OF THE CROSS (Phil. 3:2—4:1)

1. The designation of these enemies (3:2-3)
2. Paul's personal confession (3:4-14)
3. "Stand firm in the Lord" (3:15—4:1)

In this intervening passage Paul warns in a quite different vein*
against the enemies of the cross of Christ, who were working their
way into the congregation. They belonged to the circumcision
(Jews or Judaizers?) and manifested interests that were very
materialistic (3:19). In opposition to them Paul refers to his own
person and way of life. Here too he does not conceal the fact that
he once had persecuted the Christians. But the things that then
seemed essential he now considers as refuse for the sake of Christ,
who has become henceforth his only goal (3:7-14). Paul desires
the same thing for the Philippians, who were his joy and crown,
and he urges them to stand firm in the Lord (3:15—4:1).

F. FINAL ADMONITIONS AND GREETINGS
(Phil. 4:2-23)

1. Personal admonitions (4:2-3)
2. Closing admonitions and the greeting of peace (4:4-9; 3:1)
3. Gratitude for the gift from the Philippians (4:10-20)
4. Greetings and a concluding wish (4:21-23)

The closing admonition begins again with a summons to joy, a
joy that is free of care, because it knows "the Lord is nigh." Included within the good wishes for peace at the end of the letter
(vv. 9, 23) is Paul's thanksgiving for the gift from the Philippians.
He knew how to put even this within the grand context of Christ's
work. He also commends the congregation to God's care: "And
the peace of God, which passes all understanding, will keep your
hearts and your minds in Christ Jesus" (4:7).

---

*Phil. 3:1a is directly continued in 4:4.

XIII

The Letter to the Colossians

The letter to the church in Colossae, situated in the valley of the Lycus in Asia Minor, was written late in Paul's life, perhaps from Rome. The church was probably founded by disciples of Paul (cf. Epaphras—1:7). Though he did not know the congregation personally (2:1), he nevertheless felt a bond of union with it. The letter has the character of a personal address to a much greater extent than the Letter to the Ephesians.*

The letter warns against a heresy that regarded angelic forces as originators and custodians of this world order. This heresy demanded that respect be shown these forces and their regulations through an ascetic life, and through the observance of holy seasons and rules of purification. In many respects the heresy reminds one of the mystery religions (with a Jewish influence). Over against this heresy the letter asserts the sole supremacy of Christ, extending over all powers, as his dominion had become known by the Christians at baptism. Thus at the heart of the Letter to the Colossians is the baptismal confession (1:12-20), an explanation, and an exhortation founded upon it.

---

*The hypothesis that Colossians like Ephesians did not originate with Paul himself but with one of his disciples does not have as clear a basis here.

The plan of Colossians is as follows:

1:1-11	Salutation (1:1-2) Thanksgiving and intercession (1:3-11)
1:12-20	A baptismal confession concerning the redemptive work of Christ (1:12-20)
1:21-23	participated in by the church (1:21-23)
1:24-29	extended by the apostle through his ministry (1:24-29)
	Hortatory section (2:1—4:6)
2:1—4:6	Abide in what you have received and grow therein (2:1-7) Warning against false teaching (2:8-23) Christ's triumph over the powers (vv. 9-15) Admonitions on behalf of life in the name of the Lord Jesus (3:1-17; 4:5 f.) A table of Christian duties (3:18—4:1) Admonition to intercession (4:2-4)
4:7-18	Conclusion to the letter (4:7-18)

At the heart of the section concerning thanksgiving and exhortation there are descriptions of Christ's work of redemption (1:12-20; 2:9-15). According to more recent interpretation both passages were intended as a confession or hymn of the early Christian church. The former (1:12-20) was probably a baptismal confession, which Paul has here literally adopted in his letter or taken over with few alterations. If both are compared with one another, including also the hymn about Christ, in Phil. 2:5-11, then one will clearly realize how Christ's work of redemption became freely known in the early church.

In 1:12-20 Christ's redemptive work is associated with the world's creation and preservation (vv. 15-17) as well as its final redemption (vv. 19-20). (Here one is reminded of the Apostles' Creed.) In 2:9-15 his redemptive work is represented as a victory and triumph over all heavenly and earthly powers, a victory in which Christians, who are buried with Christ in baptism and raised with him, participate. Paul asserts this in view of the heresy, from which he desires to preserve the congregation. After this victory of Christ there could be no longer a dominion of any other powers "for in him the whole fulness of deity dwells bodily" (2:9).

Preceding the baptismal confession (1:12-20) are the salutation, thanksgiving, and intercessory prayer (1:1-11). Following we get a glimpse of the congregation: those who were once estranged and hostile have shared in this reconciliation (1:21-23). There is also a glimpse of the apostle's own ministry; through which he continues to carry on Christ's sufferings and glory, proclaiming the mystery that has now become manifest (1:24-29).

The hortatory section now begins. After a general admonition to abide in what they have received and to grow therein (2:1-6), the apostle warns the congregation against the heresy that is threatening it. Prior to the hymn about Christ, he labels this heresy a philosophy that is connected with elemental spirits (2:8). Then he indicates what its requirements are. Its demands, however, can have no more validity for the church that believes in Christ (2:16-23).

Following this are admonitions for the Christian life. Paul addresses the one who has been raised with Christ: "Seek the things that are above, where Christ is . . . " (3:1-4). He then gives concrete expression to this exhortation by many separate admonitions (3:5-17). These are summarized at the end by the command: "Whatever you do, in word or deed, do everything in the name of the Lord Jesus, giving thanks to God the Father through him" (3:17).

A table of duties (3:18—4:1) takes up problems pertaining to the social ranks within the congregation. At the heart of this table of duties the theme of 3:17 is once more reiterated: "Whatever your task, work heartily as serving the Lord" (3:23). Following this is an exhortation to intercessory prayer, which would include also Paul (4:2-4). This reminds one again of Paul's comment in 1:24 ff. concerning his ministry.

The end of the letter includes a good many mutual greetings. Just before the final salute is the exceedingly human and spontaneous heartfelt sigh: "Remember my fetters!"

XIV

The First Letter to the Thessalonians

First Thessalonians is the earliest letter of Paul that has been preserved to us. He wrote it several months after founding the congregation in the year 49 (2:17). Longing to see the church, he had sent Timothy there and received from him a good report (2:17—3:8). With this account fresh in mind, Paul had written the letter. This explains why it contains only a greatly amplified expression of gratitude (chs. 1—3) and an exhortation at the end of the letter (chs. 4—5).

A. THANKSGIVING (1 Thess. 1—3)

1. Salutation (1:1)
2. Thanks to God for the good standing of the congregation (1:2-10)
3. Paul's activity in Thessalonica (2:1-12)
4. Thanks for their acceptance of the word amid persecutions (2:13-16)
5. Timothy's visit (2:17—3:8)
6. A prayer that he may see them again and that the congregation may increase (3:9-13)

In a beautiful directness this letter reflects the pleasure Paul had in this congregation that had received the word with joy during much tribulation. Its faith, hope, and love were sound; and there was a good report of it in the other churches (1:2-10; 2:13-16). Paul is able also to include in this thanksgiving a grateful recollection of his ministry in Thessalonica (2:1-12). This bond with the church in Thessalonica had been of help to him in his present distressing circumstances (3:7 f.). From this expression of thanks therefore issues his prayer that he might see them again and that there might be an increase in that which God had begun there.

B. EXHORTATION (1 Thess. 4—5)

1. An admonition to continue on living in the way they have been living (4:1-2)
2. The will of God is your sanctification in modesty (4:3-8)
3. An admonition to love, to work quietly, and to command respect (4:9-12)
    Concerning those who are asleep (4:13-18)
    The day of the Lord (5:1-3)
    Admonition to vigilance and sobriety (5:4-11)
    Different admonitions (5:12-22)
4. Conclusion to the letter (5:23-28)

All the admonitions that Paul directs to the congregation in this final section are permeated with the grateful certainty that the Thessalonians have gone the right way. He can only hope that they will continue in the direction they have taken. The admonitions lack therefore a critical note. Even what he says along with the admonitions concerning the destiny of those who have fallen asleep (4:13-18) has the sound of comfort. Those who will have died before Christ's return will also be united with him. The day of his coming again may not be foreseen. He will come suddenly (5:1-3; cf. Matt. 24:42-44). The congregation can look forward to this day confidently, if they remain watchful and demonstrate self-control. "He who calls you is faithful, and he will do it" (5:24).

A chart representing the letter may be prepared as follows:

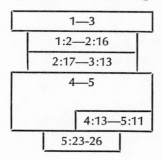

XV

The Second Letter to the Thessalonians

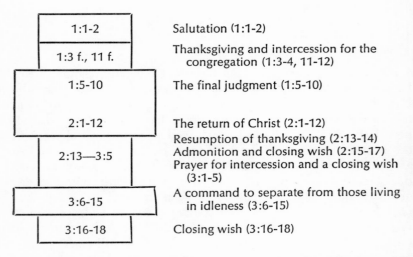

1:1-2	Salutation (1:1-2)
1:3 f., 11 f.	Thanksgiving and intercession for the congregation (1:3-4, 11-12)
1:5-10	The final judgment (1:5-10)
2:1-12	The return of Christ (2:1-12)
2:13—3:5	Resumption of thanksgiving (2:13-14) Admonition and closing wish (2:15-17) Prayer for intercession and a closing wish (3:1-5)
3:6-15	A command to separate from those living in idleness (3:6-15)
3:16-18	Closing wish (3:16-18)

After the salutation the Second Letter to the Thessalonians starts as does the first letter with thanksgiving, coming back to it later on, only to turn to it again just before the end of the letter. Similar also is the section in between, which deals with Christ's return. But 2 Thessalonians lacks the warmth and gratitude which pervade the first epistle. The expressions of thanksgiving and intercession do not sound as personal. There is also a difference in the way it mentions clearly discernible signs of Christ's return in opposition to the congregation's excited anticipation of an immediately imminent day of return (2:1-12).

In the portrayal of these signs particular stress is placed upon the judgment of the ungodly (1:5-10; 2:10-12). Before Christ's return, the adversary (or blasphemer) will come. Now, however, he is still being restrained. False conceptions concerning the end time had caused some to live in idleness. The letter warns emphatically against them (3:6-15).

Many interpreters assume that the letter was written in Paul's name by a later writer in order to preserve his heritage. At any rate it was written later than the first epistle and was addressed to a different situation.

Part Three

PASTORAL LETTERS and PHILEMON

The Pastoral Letters

Since the eighteenth century the three letters to Timothy and Titus have been looked upon as a unity under the title: "Pastoral letters." They were addressed to disciples of Paul and through them directed to a large group of congregations (in Asia Minor and Crete). Except for style and congregational situation they agree essentially in these three topics:

(1) opposition to false doctrine
(2) ecclesiastical organization
(3) exhortations

At the same time there is to be noted a distinct difference from the other Pauline letters:

a) In place of a passionate argumentation that involves itself in the arguments of the opponents, these epistles are content simply to indicate deviation from correct doctrine.
b) The ecclesiastical structure depicted here gives evidence of a later stage. Thus the offices of the ministry (bishops, elders, deacons) are thoroughly organized and define congregational life completely.
c) An atmosphere of civic uprightness is indicated in the exhortations.

By those interpreters who consider Paul to be the author of the Pastoral epistles, they are therefore placed in the last years of his life. Many expositors regard them as a pseudonymous composition, originating in Asia Minor in the second century. According to this view their supreme significance lies in the new relevance they gave to Paul's authority in the essential and basic features of his theology. This was in opposition to heresies that were invading the church at that time. They are thus a witness to the manner in which Paul's preaching became effective in an already vastly altered situation of the early church.

The First Letter to Timothy

Salutation (1:1-2)

Warning against heretics (1:3-11)

    Thanks for the service that Paul had been permitted to render (1:12-17)

Admonition to Timothy in view of the heretics (1:18-20)

    Direction on behalf of prayer in the church (2:1-15)
      The subordination of women (vv. 8-15)
    The regulation of the episcopal office (3:1-7)
    The regulation of the diaconate (3:8-13)
      Concluding with a hymn about Christ (3:14-16; 6:14-16)

Warning against the heretics (4:1-5)

    An admonition to Timothy in view of the heretics (4:6-11)
      An admonition for Timothy in connection with his office
        (4:12-16; 5:1-2)
    Regulation on behalf of widows (5:13-16)
    Regulation on behalf of elders (5:17-22)

Warning against the heretics (6:3-10)

An admonition to Timothy in view of the heretics (6:11-21)

Individual admonitions (5:23-25; 6:1-2; 6:17-19)

The plan of the epistle may be represented in chart form as follows:

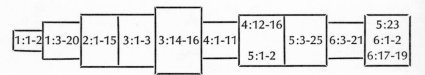

a) Warning against the heretics:

Immediately after the salutation the warning against the heretics begins, which, if not the primary object of the letter, is one of them. The warning occurs three times, followed in all three passages (chs. 1, 4, 6) by an admonition to Timothy in regard to the heretics. It thus clearly indicates that the real defense against heretics is to be sought now no longer in the congregation itself but rather in the official position—in those who hold the leading offices. At the same time the relationship between the two primary themes in the Pastoral epistles thereby becomes evident. These themes are opposition to heresy and the establishment of the ministerial offices in the church.

In 1:3-11 Timothy is distinctly commanded to oppose any different doctrine. What this is, however, is only hinted at. The fact that the teaching occupies itself with "myths," "endless genealogies," "vain discussion" and the "teaching of the law" indicates it to be a Jewish-Gnostic heresy. Over against this false doctrine the letter sets the command of love, a sincere faith, and sound doctrine.

Law is not intended for the righteous but for the lawless (note the catalogue of vices—1:9 f.).

There is a supplement in 4:1-5, indicating that the subject here concerns the heresy that had been predicted for the final age. In response to the prohibitions against certain foods which this heresy had set up the letter states that nothing created by the Lord is to be rejected, if it is received with thanksgiving.

The description of the heretics in 6:3-10 is even more ambiguous. They are reproached for manifesting "a morbid craving for controversy and for disputes about words," in addition to conceit and avarice. In contrast to this there is a reference to unpretentious "teaching which accords with godliness."

In view of the heresy Paul admonishes his son Timothy (1:18-20) to wage a good fight, by keeping faith and a good conscience. This comment is in contrast to the one concerning Hymenaeus and Alexander, who are delivered up to Satan. Thus expression is given to the fact that Timothy's office was based on Paul's ministry, for which thanks is offered in 1:12-17. This ministry rested again on the fact "that Christ Jesus came into the world to save sinners" (1:15). The section concludes with a doxology.

The admonition to Timothy in view of the heresy is continued in 4:6-11. Here he is given doctrinal authority to oppose godless, silly myths, and the superficial rules of the heretics. He is to do so with the authentic word and with good doctrine (note in v. 11: "Command and teach these things!").

In 6:11-21 Timothy is finally exhorted: "O Timothy, guard what has been entrusted to you!* Fight the good fight of faith. Take hold of the eternal life to which you were called, when you made a good confession in the presence of many witnesses" (vv. 20, 21).

Part of a hymn concerning Christ (6:14-16) is embedded within this admonition.

b) Regulations for the congregation:

These begin in 2:1-15 with directions concerning prayer in the church. Here for the first time is an exhortation to make intercession and thanksgiving on behalf of those in authority "that we may lead a quiet and peaceable life." Added in 2:9-15 is a regulation pertaining to women in the congregation. Next come the regulations for the offices of bishop and deacons (3:1-7, 8-13). In the case of both offices the provisions are of a moral rather than ecclesiastical-theological character. At the conclusion of the two passages the "mystery of our religion" is described in a hymn concerning Christ:

> "He was manifested in the flesh
> vindicated in the Spirit,
> seen by angels,
> preached among the nations,
> believed on in the world,
> taken up in glory" (3:16).

In 4:12-16 directions are given to Timothy on behalf of his office in leading the congregation (without mentioning the name of

---

*Translator's Note: Based on the author's wording, which leaves out a part of v. 12 and alters the rendering slightly.

an office). The essential feature here also is that of being an example in speech and conduct and adhering to the true faith. Scripture reading, preaching, and teaching are only mentioned.

The ecclesiastical regulations are concluded with instructions on behalf of the widows and elders. Widows (5:3-16) here belong to an ecclesiastical rank that had special duties. Those who still have a family to take care of were not to belong to this rank. Caring for a family was to take precedence (5:4-8). Younger widows were likewise to be rejected. The prerequisites for entrance into the ministry of a widow are mentioned in vv. 9 f., but nothing is said as to its exact duties. The instruction also on behalf of the elders (5:17-22) says almost nothing at all about the office.

Various individual admonitions are included in 5:23—6:2 and 6:17-19, containing comments in connection with slaves and the rich.

XVII

The Second Letter to Timothy

Second Timothy as a whole is an admonition on behalf of Timothy's ministry. It deals with (a) his preserving the piety in which he had been nurtured, (b) the challenge to follow in the path of suffering, (c) his adherence to sound doctrine, (d) his transmission of that which had been entrusted to him. Completely interwoven within this admonition is also a warning against heresy. These are the two primary motifs of the epistle. Combined with them are references to the work of Christ and the ministry of Paul, also the mention of some who have supported Paul and others who have forsaken him. These few subjects are strung together in 2 Timothy in such a loose way, however, that it is impossible to discover a meaningful arrangement for the epistle. It will be best therefore to examine it on the basis of the above-mentioned subjects. (See chart.)

The peculiarity of 2 Timothy results from its being an admonition addressed entirely to Timothy. It is therefore on the whole more highly personal than 1 Timothy. There are not any detailed congregational regulations in it. Paul's comments are also more highly subjective than objective in intent.

The challenge to follow the path of suffering is peculiar to the epistle. It is with this challenge that the exhortation proper in 1:8 begins. This readiness to suffer is in accordance with the work of Christ (1:8-10) and the example of Paul (1:11-12). In 2:3-13 the admonition is broadly expanded once more in close connection with Christ's work and Paul's example, as he says: "Take your share of suffering as a good soldier of Christ Jesus" (v. 3).

As to the other subjects, 2 Timothy resembles 1 Timothy closely. Noteworthy is the way the exhortation is founded on the faith that had come to Timothy through his grandmother and mother, even as was true of Paul (1:3-5).* Here Christian faith is viewed as a direct continuation of the Jewish faith. This indicates what a traditional concept of faith the Pastoral epistles represent.

Characteristic of 2 Timothy is finally the way in which separation between loyal and disloyal members of a congregation looms into the foreground.

Section 4:6-22 is so directly personal that it may well have been part of a letter written by Paul himself.

The following chart indicates the subjects covered in the letter.

	Ch. 1	Ch. 2	Ch. 3	Ch. 4
Salutation, thanksgiving, and intercession	1 f.			
1. Admonitions on behalf of Timothy's ministry				
a. To preserve the piety in which he had been nurtured	3-7			
b. To follow in the path of suffering	8, 12	3-13	10-12	
c. To adhere to sound doctrine	13-14	15, 22-26	14-17	
d. To transmit what had been entrusted to him		1-2		1-5
2. Warning against heresy		14, 16-18, 19-21	1-9, 13	
3. The work of Christ	8-10	8-13		
4. Paul's ministry	11-12	8-10	11	6-8, 9-18
5. Loyal and disloyal church members	15-18			10-16
Final greeting				19-22

*Translator's Note: The author's comment follows the implication of Luther's translation: "Ich danke Gott, dem ich diene *von meinen Voreltern her*" (v. 3—cf. A. V.: "whom I serve *from my forefathers*"). This is a literal rendering of the Greek *apo progonon.* Paul served God with feelings and principles derived from his parents and ancestors. Christianity to him was thus not a different religion from Judaism but its natural development (cf. Acts 23:6; 24:14). The R.S.V. rendering: "Whom I serve . . . as did my fathers" tones down this bold emphasis.

XVIII

The Letter to Titus

1. **Salutation (1:1-4)**
2. **Orders regarding elders (bishops) (1:5-9)**
3. **Warning against heretics (1:10-16)**
4. **Table of duties (2:1-10)**
   confirmed with a confession (2:11-15)
5. **Individual admonitions (3:1-2)**
   confirmed with a baptismal confession (3:3-7)
     the admonition underscored (3:8)
6. **Warning against heretics (3:9-11)**
7. **Conclusion to the letter (3:12-15)**

A chart illustrating the above outline may be constructed as follows:

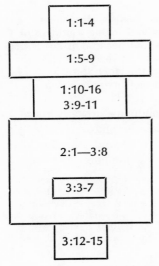

Titus resembles 1 Timothy more closely than 2 Timothy as the above survey indicates. Here one finds clearly discernible sections that are definitely related to one another. Following immediately upon the salutation are the orders regarding the elders. This applies to bishops as well (or are they the same office?) As in 1 Timothy the office has the duty of resisting heresy (cf. last clause of 1:9). There is then a description of the heresy in 1:10-16.

The table of duties (2:1-10) admonishes the older men and women and the young (only men), also slaves (not masters). The admonitions are confirmed with a summary of the Christian faith that resembles a confession:

> "For the grace of God has appeared for the salvation of all men, training us to renounce irreligion and worldly passions, and to live sober, upright, and godly lives in this world, awaiting our blessed hope, the appearing of the glory of our great God and Savior Jesus Christ, who gave himself for us to redeem us from all iniquity and to purify for himself a people of his own who are zealous for good deeds" (2:11-15).

The few individual admonitions in 3:1-2 are likewise confirmed by paraphrasing a baptismal confession:

> "For we ourselves were once foolish, disobedient, led astray . . . but when the goodness and loving kindness of God our Savior appeared, he saved us, not because of deeds done by us in righteousness, but in virtue of his own mercy, by the washing of regeneration and renewal in the Holy Spirit, which he poured out upon us richly through Jesus Christ our Savior . . . " (3:3-8)

The admonition to show obedience toward those in authority (cf. Rom. 13) is at the same time emphasized.

The letter is concluded with a second warning against heretics (3:9-12), followed by personal comments, greetings, and a final salutation (3:12-15).

XIX

The Letter to Philemon

A. Salutation (vv. 1-3)

B. Thanksgiving and an assurance of intercession (vv. 4-7)

C. A request for a friendly reception of Onesimus (vv. 8-20)

1. Paul does not wish to command but to appeal for love's sake as an old man* and a prisoner for Christ's sake (vv. 8-19)

2. Concerning Onesimus, whom Paul had begotten in the faith during his imprisonment (vv. 10-11)

3. Paul is sending him back in order not to retain him in his own service without Philemon's consent (vv. 12-14)

4. Onesimus has now become a brother to Philemon (vv. 15-16)

5. Paul asks for a friendly reception and desires to make amends for any damages that have originated with Philemon (vv. 17-20)

---

*Translator's Note: Following the German rendering (cf. RSV margin). The Greek term used here is *presbutes*, which means literally "old man." The term is derived from the Greek verb *presbeuein* "to be an elder (or an ambassador)" (cf. 2 Cor. 5:20; Eph. 6:2). RSV has adopted this latter sense in its rendering.

D. Conclusion to the letter (vv. 21-25)

> Paul has written this way with confidence in Philemon. He hopes
> for a speedy reunion, extends greetings, and concludes: "The
> grace of the Lord Jesus Christ be with your spirit."

In chart form the letter may be represented as follows:

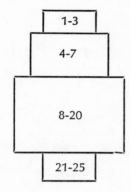

Part Four

REMAINING EPISTLES

The Letter to the Hebrews

Hebrews is a comforting, hortatory, and explanatory message to a congregation (or group) that was in danger of drifting away (2:1). They were depressed and subject to temptation (3:6, 14; 10:35; 12:12). The epistle urges them to hold fast to their confession (4:14). This is done in such a way that Christ's greatness is set before them from the first to the last sentence. This magnifying of Christ occurs through the exposition of a series of Old Testament expressions and associations, all of which are intended to prove the superiority of the person and work of Christ. The pilgrim people of God experience strength and guidance to the extent that Christ becomes great to them. In this way they are directed to their destination—rest at the end of their pilgrimage.

The title "to the Hebrews" was not given to the epistle until a later date. The book begins without any salutation. Only the conclusion (13:18-25) has the evident character of an epistle. Nothing is known concerning either the author or the ones to whom it is addressed. The letter did not come into the canon until later. Its essential significance lies in its exposition of the office of Jesus Christ as the ultimate fulfillment of the Old Testament priesthood and sacrificial ministry.

Prologue: God's Final Word (1:1-4)

God has spoken his final word in his Son, whom he has exalted to his right hand after his work of redemption

A. THE SUPERIORITY OF CHRIST (Heb. 1:5—4:13)

1. According to the Scriptures Christ has been exalted above the angels (1:5-14)
   An admonition to heed this word (2:1-4)
2. Because of his suffering he was glorified (Ps. 8) (2:5-10)
3. He has become our brother in order to deliver us (2:11-18)
4. As Son he is also elevated above Moses (3:1-6)
5. Warning against unbelief (Ps. 95:7-11) (3:7—4:13)

B. IN CHRIST THE PRIESTLY MINISTRY AND OFFERING ARE FULFILLED (Heb. 4:14—10:18)

1. We have a high priest who sympathizes with us (4:14-16)
2. We have a high priest who has been appointed and confirmed by God (Ps. 2) (5:1-10)
3. The weak congregation, the bold promise (5:11—6:20)
4. Christ, a priest according to the order of Melchizedek (7:1-28)
   a. The priesthood of Melchizedek, which is superior to that of the Levites (7:1-10)
   b. The Levitical priesthood is annulled by Christ (7:11-24)
   c. This he has done *once for all* (7:25-28)
5. Christ, the mediator of a *new* covenant (Jer. 31) (8:1-13)
6. The old and new access to the sanctuary (9:1-28)
   a. The access to the old sanctuary (9:1-10)
   b. The access by Christ's own blood (9:11-22)
   c. Once for all (9:23-28)
7. The sacrifice of Christ once for all (10:1-18)

C. ADMONITION: "LET US NOW DRAW NEAR!" (Heb. 10:19—13:17)

1. Let us hold fast to the confession of our hope (10:19-25)
2. Backsliders will fall under judgment (10:26-31)
3. Do not cast away your confidence (10:32-39)
4. *The history of faith* (11:1-40)
5. Let us look to the pioneer and perfecter of our faith! (12:1-3)
6. Discipline, a sign of fatherly love (12:4-11)
7. Admonitions to endure (12:12-29)
8. Various admonitions (13:1-17)
9. Conclusion to the letter (13:18-25)

The above may be expressed in chart form as follows:

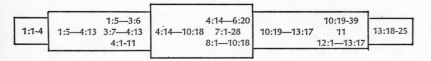

| 1:1-4 | 1:5—4:13 | 1:5—3:6
3:7—4:13
4:1-11 | 4:14—10:18 | 4:14—6:20
7:1-28
8:1—10:18 | 10:19—13:17 | 10:19-39
11
12:1—13:17 | 13:18-25 |

Hebrews is arranged in three carefully planned sections:

(1) The first section describes the superiority of Jesus Christ (1:1—4:13) but includes at the same time the theme that leads to the second section; this supreme being has stooped down to become our brother.

(2) The middle section (4:14—10:18) tells about his work of salvation on our behalf presented from the standpoint of the Old Testament. It shows how the office of the priesthood and sacrifice reached their fulfillment in Christ, who has thereby provided the entrance into the sanctuary.

(3) The third section (10:19—13:17) then issues the summons to enter, to accept Christ's saving work, to hold fast the acknowledgment of him.

With this the most important features of the book have been designated. To understand Hebrews, however, it is essential to note a further bond that holds everything together, viz., the concept of *the word,* under which is included Christ's complete work of salvation in the prologue (1:1-4). Christ is God's ultimate word to the world. Matching this in ch. 11 is the grand summons to *faith* in the recital of the story of those who have believed that Christ is the ultimate word of God to the world. In this very way he is the "pioneer and perfecter of our faith" (12:2).

Prologue: God's Final Word (Heb. 1:1-4)

Ch. 1:1-4 has the character of a prologue. In a few words the entire saving work of Christ is described with emphasis on his exaltation. In this work God has spoken through his Son. This is God's absolute final word, although it is not his initial word; for "in many and various ways God spoke of old to our fathers." The Letter to the Hebrews has to do with the relationship between the ultimate and preparatory word.

A. THE SUPERIORITY OF JESUS CHRIST (Heb. 1:5—4:13)

The superiority of Christ over the angels (1:5-14) as well as Moses (3:1-6) can be demonstrated in the Scriptures (the former in Psalms 2, 110, etc.; the latter by virtue of his name as Son). Between these two sections (in 2:5-18) the exaltation of Christ is linked with his humiliation. He was "crowned with glory and honor because of the suffering of death (2:9). For "it was fitting that he . . . should make the pioneer of their salvation perfect through suffering" (2:5-10). The same is indicated in 2:11-18 from the human aspect. He became our brother in his work of salvation (Ps. 22:23). "Therefore he had to be made like his brethren in every respect" (2:17).

Following both sections, which demonstrate Christ's superiority over the angels and over Moses, there is an admonition in each case to submit to this supreme power (2:1-4 and 3:7—4:13). In 3:7 ff. this occurs in an exposition of Ps. 95:7-11: "Today, when you hear his voice, do not harden your hearts. . . . "

God's pilgrim people of the new covenant are reminded of the people of the old covenant (3:15-18) and through them warned against being left behind, falling into unbelief, and missing the goal, namely, rest at the end of the road. The first part concludes with a warning reference to the vital power of God's word (4:12; cf. 1:2).

B. THE FULFILLMENT OF THE PRIESTLY MINISTRY AND OFFERING IN CHRIST (Heb. 4:14—10:18)

The two prerequisites for the work of salvation are placed at the beginning in 4:14—5:10 as an introduction. It states that we have a high priest who can sympathize with us, because he was tempted in every respect as we are (4:13-16 and 5:7-8). Christ, however, did not assume the dignity of his high priestly office on his own behalf. It was rather bestowed on him by God, as indicated in Pss. 2 and 110, which are interpreted as referring to Christ.

Ch. 7:1 ff. is directly connected with 5:10. First comes an important parenthetical section (5:11—6:20), which is intended to prepare for the real heart of the letter in chs. 7—10, by providing a glimpse of those it is addressing. They are really not yet in a position to comprehend what is being said (5:11-14). Nevertheless the author wants to speak to them about these great concerns, "convinced," as he says, "that you are near to salvation" * (6:9). (The "therefore" in 6:1 is significant.)

In the midst of this section (6:1-10) there is a rejection of a second repentance for those who have once become apostate (vv. 4-8). The rejection stands in the sharpest contrast to this nearness to salvation. On this point, for example, Luther has sharply opposed the Letter to the Hebrews.

The conclusion of the parenthetical section (6:11-20) adopts again the admonition of 4:14: patient endurance will surely be rewarded. God by an oath has made himself dependent on his promise (Gen. 22:16 ff.).

In chs. 7—10 Christ's work of salvation is developed from two aspects:

(1) Christ is high priest according to the order of Melchizedek (chs. 7—8). This concept is based on Ps: 110:4 (Heb. 5:6; 6:20) and is depicted according to Gen. 14 in 7:1-10, which points out

---

*Translator's Note: Based on the German wording. A literal rendering of the original Greek would be: "We are persuaded of better things of you, and that belong to salvation." Compare the rendering of the New English Bible: "We are convinced that you . . . are in the better care, and this makes for your salvation."

his superiority to the Levitical priesthood. Insofar as the priesthood of Melchizedek rested on an oath of God (Ps. 110:4), Jesus also has become the guarantee of a better covenant (7:11-28). Ch. 8 amplifies this in greater detail, citing fully in this connection the proof passage (Jer. 31:31-34).

(2) In chs. 9—10 the new worship service is contrasted with the old one. The separation of the Holy Place from Holy of Holies was characteristic of the ancient sanctuary. There was also no open access in the sacrificial ministry of the high priest; for he had to offer sacrifices there for the sins of the people year by year (9:1-10). Christ, however, entered into the sanctuary *once* through his own blood, a sanctuary not made indeed with hands but one that is eternal—even heaven. The link with the old worship lies simply in the fact that purification from sins is possible only by means of blood in this sanctuary as well as that one (9:11-28). The emphasis in this connection lies on the uniqueness of the sacrifice. Ch. 10:1-18 further underscores this. The superiority of Christ's sacrifice is, moreover, demonstrated by the fact that there were allusions already in the Old Testament to the limitation of animal sacrifice (Ps. 40:6-8; 51:16). This section also concludes with a reference to the promise of a new covenant in Jer. 31.

C. ADMONITION: "LET US NOW DRAW NEAR"
(Heb. 10:19—13:17)

The final section in 10:19-25 adopts again the introductory admonition of the central section (10:23 = 4:14), summing up this central section in vv. 19-21 and leading on to the single exhortation of vv. 24-25. This is founded on a threat (10:26-31) and a promise (10:32-39). In the threat there is a denial again of a possibility for a second repentance, coupled with the warning: "It is a fearful thing to fall into the hands of the living God" (10:31). In the promise, which recalls the suffering that had already been endured, there is encouragement in view of eternity: "Do not throw away your confidence, which has a great reward" (10:35).

In order to cheer those who are depressed, the writer now directs their attention to the "cloud of witnesses" (ch. 11). He depicts the whole history of God's people under the old covenant as a history of faith, stressing in the last section (vv. 35-38) how they suffered for their faith during this period. If one reads this chapter carefully sentence by sentence, one will realize to what extent the Christian community, where this letter arose and circulated, lived in the Old Testament. They understood the history of the old covenant as God's history.

The admonition to hold fast (10:19-25) is again picked up in 12:1-3 with a reference to the goal of this history that has been portrayed in ch. 11: "Let us look to Jesus the pioneer and perfecter of our faith!" In view of his suffering, the discipline experienced by those who follow him can also be accepted as a sign of fatherly love (12:4-11). "Therefore lift your drooping hands," he says, "and strengthen your weak knees" (12:12).

In this way the writer introduces the concluding admonitions of the letter (12:12-17), contrasting at the same time the revelation at Sinai with that of the heavenly Jerusalem (12:18-29). At the center of these admonitions (13:1-17) stands the statement: "Jesus Christ is the same yesterday and today and forever" (13:18), summing up in a monumental way the work of Christ.

XXI

The Letter of James

This letter is a didactic and hortatory composition (parenesis), which addresses a Christian community that has become indifferent and careless. (This is what is meant by the reference to "the twelve tribes in the Dispersion," 1:1.) It desires to summon them to an earnest, wholehearted obedience. The epistolary style is here simply a literary device. There is nothing at all concrete or specific mentioned about the situation of the congregations to which it is addressed.

The almost complete absence of comment regarding the basic facts of salvation is especially noteworthy. (This is rather in contrast to 1 Peter.) The name of Christ is hardly ever mentioned.

The admonitions are ranged one after the other without any obvious connection. A basic characteristic, however, may be discerned in the frequent reference to showing the reality of one's faith.

1. Salutation (1:1)
2. Proof through testing (1:2-18)
3. "Be doers of the word and not hearers only" (1:19-27)
4. Do not despise the poor (2:1-13)
5. "Faith without works is dead" (2:14-26)
6. A warning against pressing toward the office of teaching; the power of the tongue (3:1-12)
7. Warning against selfish ambition (3:13-18)
8. Friendship with the world is enmity with God (4:1-10)
9. Warning against slander and false security (4:11-17)
10. An accusation against the rich (5:1-6)

11. "Be patient!" (5:7-11)
12. Various admonitions (5:12-20)

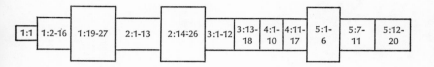

| 1:1 | 1:2-16 | 1:19-27 | 2:1-13 | 2:14-26 | 3:1-12 | 3:13-18 | 4:1-10 | 4:11-17 | 5:1-6 | 5:7-11 | 5:12-20 |

The Epistle of James advocates what one today would call "practical Christianity." He apparently had no interest whatsoever in theology as such. The letter contains no trace of concern about the peril of heresy. For him the danger lay solely in the imperfect or perverse behavior of Christians.

In 2:14-26 the letter opposes an attitude that appeals to faith so as to avoid behaving obediently. It speaks out openly at this point against a misunderstood or distorted Pauline teaching and (using Abraham's example) draws a conclusion that is the reverse of Paul's in Rom. 4. Luther's antipathy to James is to be understood entirely from this standpoint.

We should bear in mind, moreover, that James was speaking in a situation that had altered and in regard to a corrupted Paulinism. But he himself also seems no longer to have had an appreciation for that which Paul meant, even though his call to prove one's faith by one's conduct is entirely correct as such.

In 2:1-13 special emphasis is placed upon intercession for the poor; and 5:1-6 stresses the indictment of the rich. These passages assume that social differences were beginning to become a threat within Christianity in the time of the Letter of James (ca. 100 A.D.). The comment of James at this point is a sincere and courageous call to repentance, even as is his warning against selfish ambition and every form of disagreement (3:13-18). The observations concerning the power of the tongue (3:1-12) remind one specifically of Old Testament wisdom,* which may be noted also in other comments.

---

*Translator's Note: Cf. Westermann, *op. cit.,* pp. 237 ff.

XXII

The First Letter of Peter

The letter was addressed to congregations in Asia Minor and was written probably from Rome [Babylon] (5:13). It is a moot question as to whether the apostle Peter was the author. Many expositors assume that it was written by Silvanus (mentioned in 5:12) under the authority of Peter.

Immediately after the salutation (1:1-2) and the glorification of God (1:3-12), it begins with exhortation and remains a hortatory address to the end of the letter (5:12-14). Inserted repeatedly in the admonitions are passages of a hymn-like or confessional character, speaking of Christ and his work. There are also detailed references to the Old Testament. A pervasive motif within the admonitions is the summons to be ready for suffering and connected with this readiness to suffer is the comforting promise.

Salutation (1 Peter 1:1-2)

A. The Glorification of God (1 Peter 1:3-12)

1. "Born anew to a living hope" (1:3-5)
2. Tested by the fire of tribulation (1:6-9)
3. The prophets alluded to this fulfillment (1:10-12)

B. An Admonition to Holy Conduct and Brotherly Love (1 Peter 1:13-25)

1. "Gird up your minds" (1:13-17)
2. You have been dearly bought (Christ's work) (1:18-21)
3. "Love one another ... from the heart" (1:22)
4. Born anew through the living word (1:23-25. Cf. Isa. 40:6-8)

C. "Come to Him, to that Living Stone" (1 Peter 2:1-10

1. A call to a completely new beginning (2:1-3)
2. Established in the promise of Isa. 28:16, which has now been fulfilled: "You are . . . a holy nation" (Ex. 19 f.*) (2:4-10)

D. Exhortations Concerning Social Rank (1 Peter 2:11—3:7)

1. "Maintain good conduct among the Gentiles" (2:11-12)
2. Admonition to those in authority about obedience (2:13-17)
   (2:13-17)
3. An admonition to slaves (2:18-25)
   Christ died for you! (vv. 21-25. Cf. Isa. 53)
4. An admonition for married couples (3:1-7)

E. General Exhortations, Particularly on Behalf of Suffering (1 Peter 3:8—5:9)

1. Seek peace and pursue it (3:8-12. Cf. Ps. 34:13-17)
2. Blessed are those who endure suffering (3:13-17)
3. The work of Christ, appropriated in baptism (3:18-22)
   Also on behalf of the dead (3:19 f.; 4:6)
4. The life that has thereby been changed (4:1-6)
5. Various admonitions (The end is near) (4:7-11)
6. Rejoice, you who suffer as Christians (4:12-19)
7. An admonition to the old (5:1-4)
8. An admonition to the young: "Be sober, be watchful. Your adversary . . . " (5:5-9)

F. A Conclusion to the Letter (1 Peter 5:10-14)

1. "The God of all grace . . . will . . . " (5:10-11)
2. Final word. Greetings. Salutation of peace (5:12-14)

In chart form the epistle may be represented as follows:

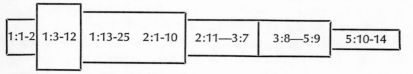

*Translator's Note: Specifically Ex. 19:6.

In the eulogy of God at the outset (1:3-12) there are allusions to all the basic themes of the letter:

1. The new birth

God is glorified for that which he has done for us in Christ. He has caused us to be born anew to a living hope (1:3-5). In 1:23-25 the first section returns again to this reference "born anew."

The next part issues a call to a new beginning on the basis of the promise that has now been fulfilled (2:1-10) and expressly designates baptism as this new beginning (3:19-22). (1 Peter 4:1-6 with its account of the changed life agrees with this.) In view of this theme that decidedly dominates 1 Peter, one is tempted to conceive of the entire letter as a baptismal sermon or an exhortation concerning baptism. But this would be perhaps too limited a concept, because it is the church and really not an individual Christian that is being addressed throughout the entire letter. Nevertheless, a fundamental theme in the hortatory message of 1 Peter is the new birth, which is attested in baptism.

This new birth is made possible "through the resurrection of Jesus Christ from the dead" (1:3-5). The church confesses this faith, and the apostle calls it to mind when he says: "You were ransomed . . . with the precious blood of Christ" (1:18-21). He reminds slaves especially of this when he says: "Christ also suffered for you, leaving an example for you to follow . . . " (2:21-25). Then follows again at this point a description of Christ's work of salvation, echoing the promise of Isa. 53.

There is a further summary of this work of salvation in 3:18-22, linked with the call to be prepared to suffer (3:13-17). In many of its phrases this already reminds one distinctly of the Apostles' Creed. Here also is the passage that formed the basis for the phrase: "he descended into hell" (3:19 f.; 4:6).

2. The proof of faith through suffering

Proving faith through suffering (1:6-9) is the second all-pervading motif. In this connection the hortatory material has in every respect the sound of friendly, encouraging comfort. This is especially so in 3:13-17, where it makes use of the beatitude about those who suffer (cf. v. 14). Above all this is called to mind probably in connection with persecutions. But the admonition in 2:19-21 addressed to slaves indicates that every kind of suffering was being considered in addition to this. How important this very aspect of Christian existence was to the apostle is understood in paragraph 4:12-19. Here, after a preliminary concluding statement, he takes up once more this comforting exhortation in detail. The name "Christian" occurs only here* and in Acts 11:26; 26:28.

Finally the last admonition, addressed to the young men, refers to the way suffering is a part of Christian existence: "Be sober, be watchful . . . knowing that the same experience of suffering is required of your brotherhood throughout the world" (5:8 f.).

3. The promise of the Old Testament

The salvation granted to Christians, which now has been revealed, is based on the promise of the Old Testament, especially the prophets (1:10-12). This reference to the Old Testament runs throughout the entire letter:

(a) The living word which effects a new birth (1:23 ff.) is the subject of the prologue of Isa. 40:1-11.

(b) The exhortation "Be yourselves built into a spiritual house" (2:1-10) is based on the comment concerning the cornerstone in Isa. 28:4-22, also Ex. 19:5 f.

(c) The confession concerning Christ in 2:21-25 is based on the Song of the Suffering Servant in Isa. 53.

(d) And the general admonition in 3:8-12 cites Ps. 34:13-17. These are only the most important and obvious Old Testament contexts to which 1 Peter makes reference. At the same time it should be noted that this occurs in all the above-mentioned passages without any artificiality or reinterpretation. Each of these Old Testament utterances can be understood today in exactly the same way.

It is unnecessary to enlarge upon the way hortatory material is developed in individual passages, because it corresponds exactly to this kind of material in other letters.

---

*If one suffers as a Christian . . . " (4:16).

XXIII

The Second Letter of Peter and the Letter of Jude

A. Salutation (2 Peter 1:1-2)

B. An Admonition to Increase and Promote Godliness
   (2 Peter 1:3-11)

C. A Testament in View of Impending Death (2 Peter 1:12-15)

D. Concerned with the Return of Christ (2 Peter 1:16-21)

E. An Announcement about Heretics (2 Peter 2:1-3; cf. Jude 4)
   (Note the correspondences with Jude 3-18)
   1. Heretics will arise and get a great following (2:1-3. Cf. Jude 4)
   2. God will punish them in accordance with the former judgment
      2:4-9. Cf. Jude 5-7)
   3. They blaspheme even the angels (2:10-11. Cf. Jude 8-10)
   4. They commit every base act (2:12-16. Cf. Jude 11)
   5. The depraved return to their own filth (2:17-22. Cf. Jude 12-16)

F. The Return of Christ (2 Peter 3:1-18)
   1. The question of the scoffers: What delays the return? (3:1-4)
   2. The catastrophe of the flood at the beginning corresponds to the
      catastrophe of fire in the final age (3:5-7)
   3. His delay is due to his longsuffering
      (" . . . a thousand years as one day") (3:8-9)
   4. The day of the Lord will come like a thief (3:10)
   5. Prepare yourselves for the final age! (3:11-15)
   6. The delay is our salvation, even as Paul says (3:15-16)
   7. Final admonition and doxology (3:17-18)

The outline may be expressed in the form of a chart as follows:

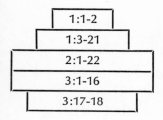

Almost all expositors assign 2 Peter to a later period. It has a style that has Hellenistic features (e.g., the reference to "partakers of the divine nature" in 1:4, the concept of virtue in 1:5). It already presupposes that there is a canon of Pauline letters, to which heretics are falsely appealing. It also reproduces Jude 3-18 in ch. 2.

The purpose of the letter was to certify that Christ's second coming was true. This was in opposition to the gnostic heretics, who are described in ch. 2. The heretics asked jeeringly: "What then is delaying the return?" The epistle of 2 Peter sets God over against this ridicule, God with whom a thousand years are as a day. The delay that he still permits is for our salvation. All apostles concur in this (he says) even Paul, whose writings are difficult to understand in many respects. Apparently the heretics were appealing to them.

The day of the Lord will come as a thief (cf. Matt. 24:43 f.). It is well to prepare oneself for this day.

THE LETTER OF JUDE

1. Salutation (vv. 1-2)
2. Exhortation to contend for the traditional faith (v. 3)
3. The heretics (vv. 4-16)
   foretold by the apostles (vv. 17-19)
4. Admonition: "Build yourselves up on your most holy faith" (vv. 20-23)
5. Doxology (vv. 24-25)

XXIV

The First Letter of John

A salutation is missing in 1 John. This has been replaced by a prologue. The letter is a hortatory tract, written to a congregation or group of congregations that were in danger of the inroad of heresy. This is clearly designated as a gnostic heresy in 2:18-27. The heretics were denying that Christ (whom they perhaps also acknowledged) was the real man Jesus (4:2 f.). They considered themselves as perfect and sinless (1:10) and believed that they were therefore not bound to obey commandments (2:4).

The points at which the heretics were making their attack furnish the primary themes of the letter. On this basis it is also clear that the prologue was apparently a restatement of John 1:14. The incarnation was at the heart of the faith, under attack by the heretics.

The prologue and style of the whole letter resemble the Gospel of John to such an extent that it is quite likely that they stem from the same author or at any rate the same theological group. This is also true of the second and third letters of John, which are to be recognized more evidently as real letters.

Prologue: We Testify to the Word of Life (1 John 1:1-4)

A. The Message of Light (1 John 1:5—2:17)

    1. Walk in the light—confess sin (1:5—2:2)
    2. Know God—keep his commandments (2:3-6)
    3. The old-new commandment of brotherly love (2:7-11)
    4. "You know the Father" (2:12-17)

B. Warning Against the Message of the Antichrists (1 John 2:18-29)

1. "Children, it is the last hour!" (2:18-19)
2. You know the truth and the liar (2:20-23)
   "He who denies that Jesus is the Christ" (v. 22)
3. Abide in what you have heard from the beginning (2:24-29)

C. Abide in God—Abide in Love (1 John 3:1-24)

1. He who abides in him does not sin (3:1-10)
2. He who does not love remains in death (3:11-18)
3. He who keeps his commandments abides in him.
   "God is greater than our heart" (3:19-24)

D. Warning Against the Heretics (1 John 4:1-6)

E. God Is Love—Let Us Love (1 John 4:7-21)

F. Our Faith Overcomes the World in Love (1 John 5:1-5)

G. The Testimony to Christ by the Spirit, the Water, and the Blood (1 John 5:6-12)

H. Conclusion to the Letter: Assured That Our Prayers Are Heard (1 John 5:13-15)

Supplement: Mortal sin and sin which is not mortal (5:16-21)

The outline may be expressed in chart form as follows:

1:1-4	1:5—2:17	2:18-29 / 4:1-6	3:1-24	4:7-21	5:1-12	5:13-15	5:16-21

The highly individualistic style of this letter is only to be understood in relation to and on the basis of the Gospel. There are really only a few declarations and challenges that extend in a kaleido-scopic manner throughout the entire letter. They continually receive a slightly different turn and keep on appearing in a different interrelationship toward one another. The distinct individuality of the Johannine style, which expresses itself in paradoxical contrasts, is a part of this. These paradoxes are employed in ever new ways so that the reader is again and again startled by the surprising shades of meaning and the purely logical contradictions between two statements that conflict in wording with one another. An example of this is the contradiction between 1:8 and 3:6. What sin signifies to those who believe can only be expressed in such a paradoxical fashion.

XXV

The Second and Third Letters of John

"The Elder" is designated as the sender of both letters. The epistle of 2 John is addressed to the congregation; 3 John to an individual named Gaius.

After the salutation (vv. 1-3), thanksgiving, and intercession (vv. 4-6),* 2 John warns against the same heretics as does 1 John (2:18-29) and demands a strict separation from them (vv. 7-11). In the conclusion to his letter (vv. 12-13) the Elder announces his impending visit.

The epistle of 3 John lauds Gaius for his reception of the brethren (vv. 3-8) and rebukes Diotrephes, who has failed to do so and has refused to recognize the writer of the letter (vv. 9-10). Diotrephes was perhaps the representative of an episcopal administration of the congregation that opposed the charismatic itinerant apostle. (Cf. the phrase in v. 9: "who likes to put himself first.") The conclusion to the letter (vv. 13-15) is quite similar to that of 2 John.

The epistles may be charted as follows:

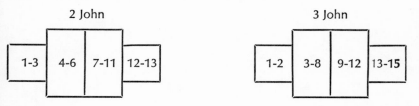

2 John

| 1-3 | 4-6 | 7-11 | 12-13 |

3 John

| 1-2 | 3-8 | 9-12 | 13-15 |

---

*This is entirely in the style of 1 John.

Part Five

AN APOCALYPSE

The Revelation to John

XXVI

The Revelation to John

The Revelation to John belongs to the important literary group of apocalypses, of which there were very many in late Judaism. The second half of the Book of Daniel, the little apocalypse of Isaiah (chs. 24–27), and the vision of Zechariah (chs. 1–6) belong to this group. Many portions of Ezekiel also include apocalyptic features. In the New Testament the "Synoptic apocalypses" should be set alongside it (see above, pp. 25, 33, 46).

The peculiar character of Revelation is derived from the way it combines the visions of the final age (chs. 4–22) with the Seven Letters to the Churches in the province of Asia* (chs. 2–3). Both are preceded by the account of the call (ch. 1). The whole book is introduced (1:4) and concluded (22:21) as a letter and is accordingly intended as an address to the churches. In a period when persecution was on the rise the churches were to be strengthened and comforted by being shown the vast context in which their present time of vexation stood, also by a reference to the objective of these powerful movements, viz., the ultimate victory of Jesus Christ at the time of his return to judge and redeem.

The Apocalypse was written toward the end of the first century according to the prevailing opinion of scholars. Whether the writer was the apostle, an Asia Minor presbyter, or an unknown John has been a controversial question since ancient times. There was also a long dispute over the admission of the Apocalypse into

---

*Translator's Note: A small Roman province in Asia Minor, bounded on the north by Bithynia, on the east by Galatia, on the south by Pamphylia and Lycia, and on the east by the Aegean Sea. The term "Asia" in the New Testament never refers to the continent that is known by that name.

the New Testament canon. Its significance as a whole in the New Testament lies above all in the fact that the Christ event is here set within the widest possible temporal and spacial compass.

A chart for the book may be prepared as follows:

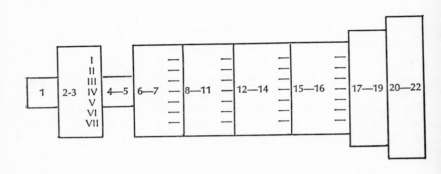

A. THE VISION CONCERNING THE CALL OF THE SEER JOHN (Rev. 1:1-20)

1. An expanded superscription (1:1-3)
2. The introduction to the letter, expanded into a doxology (1:4-8)
3. The vision of the call on the island of Patmos (1:9-20)
   a. Introduction: John, exiled to Patmos (1:9)
   b. The commission to the Seven Churches (1:10, 11, 19 f.)
   c. The vision of the Son of man (1:12-16)
   d. "Fear not, I am ... " (1:17-18)

The vision of the seer John at the time of his call (1:9-20) brings to mind in one feature after the other the calls of the prophets (cf. Isa. 6; Jer. 1; Ezek. 1–3). In this vision God (or the exalted Christ) in his holiness encounters man. The man is frightened to death in the presence of this manifestation and hears within the vision the assurance "Fear not!" that extends throughout the entire Bible. His commission issues out of this encounter (cf. the arrangement of Isa. 6).*

In this encounter the *real*, absolutely basic revelation is contained: Christ reveals himself, declaring, "I am the first and the last, and the living one . . ." (1:17 f.).†

The entire Book of Revelation is simply an unfolding of this self-revelation of Christ. In the commission (v. 19, appropriating the language of vv. 10, 11), which comes after this revelation, there then also follows immediately a summary of the whole book, viz.:

Write

what you see = ch. 1: the vision at the call

what is = chs. 2—3: the circular letters

what is to take place = chs. 4—22: the view of the future

B. THE SEVEN LETTERS (Rev. 2—3)

1. The church in Ephesus (2:1-7)
2. The church in Smyrna (2:8-11)
3. The church in Pergamum (2:12-17)
4. The church in Thyatira (2:18-29)
5. The church in Sardis (3:1-6)
6. The church in Philadelphia (3:7-13)
7. The church in Laodicea (3:14-22)

All these open letters to the Seven Churches include the same basic features:

In the light of the current condition of the churches, there is laudatory recognition and stern rebuke. ("I know your works . . . but I have this against you.") The comments are different in respect to each of the congregations. These vary from rather slight rebuke (Pergamum) to exceedingly harsh criticism (Laodicea). Only in

---

*Translator's Note: See Westermann, *op. cit.*, pp. 135 f.

†The doxology of the salutation in 1:4-8 is on a par with this.

the case of Smyrna is praise and blame entirely lacking. Here only the affliction of the congregation is singled out.

In terms of the future the letters contain announcements concerning the further destiny of the churches, an admonition to repent. Included are threats of judgment in the case of some. All end, however, with promises of salvation. Running through all of them is the call to perseverance and faithfulness: "Be faithful unto death, and I will give you the crown of life" (2:10; likewise 3:11). The One who speaks in these messages to the churches is Christ himself. The description of the exalted One in the vision of ch. 1 is borrowed for the introductory words in each case.

C. THE REVELATION (Rev. 4—22)

1. The vision of the throne: the One enthroned and the lamb (4—5)
2. The seven seals (6—7)
3. The seven trumpets (8—11)
4. Interlude: The scroll and the staff (10:1—11:14)
5. The drama of the final age (12—14)
6. The seven bowls (15—16)
7. Judgment and victory over Babylon (17—19)
8. The reign of peace and the new Jerusalem (20—22)

The continuity and significance of this vast literary scheme in the revelation granted to John are extremely complicated. It has been interpreted up to the present time also in quite different ways. The few lines of thought indicated here can therefore only be an attempt.

The vision of the throne in chs. 4 and 5 is introductory in character. Everything the seer has to announce issues from his encounter with God, who is the Lord in his majesty (ch. 4) and in his compassion (ch. 5). The vision of this One who was enthroned corresponds even in details with Isa. 6 and Ezek. 1. At the heart of the account is the adoration of God's majesty by the heavenly beings. This conforms with Isa. 6: "Holy, holy, holy . . ." The scroll fastened with seven seals, which he holds in his hand, indicates the divine plan that encompasses world history. The mystery of history, however, is hidden. (This is indicated by the seven seals.) The sorrow of all living creatures, during the period God's activity in history remains hidden, is suggested by the weeping of the seer (5:4). The mystery would have remained forever concealed, if the Lamb (Christ in his conquest through his suffering and death—5:9 f.) had not opened the scroll. Therefore Christ and his work are now included in the praise of God. All creatures at the end shout with joy, saying: "To him who sits upon the throne and to the Lamb be blessing and honor and glory and might forever and ever" (5:13).

For an understanding of that which is to follow one must assume that an ancient document frequently consisted of two parts. These included an open section for anyone to read and a sealed section. (So Bornkamm and others.*) The visions of the seven seals (chs. 6—7) present the one section of the scroll (5:1). They are the prelude to the actual disclosure of the document by the opening of the seventh seal in 8:1. "When the Lamb opened the seventh seal, there was silence in heaven. . . ."

What now follows in 8:2—22:21 is the disclosing of the seven-sealed scroll to the seer, beginning with the seven trumpet visions (chs. 8—11). With the sounding of the trumpets the final judgment begins. Whereas the first six trumpets (chs. 8—9) announce the various acts of destructive judgment, the seventh trumpet indicates the other aspect, viz., the coming of eternal salvation (11:15-19). But an interlude between the sixth and seventh trumpet visions (10:1—11:14) vividly links the history of God's people with that which is to take place in the final age. In this section a more important interlude, quite complete in itself (chs. 12—14), is introduced. In powerful, fabulous imagery the destiny and history of God's people is connected intimately with the deeds of the end time. The woman in ch. 12 represents the people of God; her child is the Messiah; the dragon and the two beasts of ch. 12 f. are the world powers that threaten to destroy the people of God.

---

*Bornkamm, G., "Studien zu Antike und Urchristentum," *Beiträge zur evangelischen Theologie,* Vol. 28 (1959), pp. 221 f.; Staritz, K., "Zu Offenbarung 5:1," *Zeitschrift für die Neutestamentliche Wissenschaft,* Vol. 30 (1931), pp. 157 ff.

As regards the final history, the story of God's people is sketched along broad, quite limited lines in chs. 12—14.

The seven visions concerning the bowls of wrath now follow in chs. 15—16. These are poured out over the world that is in rebellion against God. It should be observed in this connection that these visions correspond exactly even as to detail with the seven trumpet visions. This is intended to indicate that a fixed succession has not been observed here but rather a mysterious interplay of events.

The Seven Trumpets		The Seven Seals
Preparation	8:2-6	15:1-5; 16:1
First	8:7	16:2
Second	8:8 f.	16:3
Third	8:10 f.	16:4 (-7)
Fourth	8:12	16:8 f.
Fifth	9:1 f.	10:10 f.
Sixth	9:14 f.	16:12 (-16)
Seventh	11:15-19	16:17 (-21)

Only in chs. 17—19 does the final act begin. The world power, opposed to Christ, is portrayed in the "great harlot Babylon," who rises to dreadful heights. John declares: "I saw the woman drunk with the blood of the saints and with the blood of the martyrs of Jesus" (ch. 17). She is then hurled down from her high position (ch. 18), as the angel calls out: "Fallen, fallen is Babylon the great . . . " (cf. Isa. 21:9). The account pictures the way the entire world, above all trade and commerce, is affected by the overthrow of this world power. (In ch. 18:11-17a the merchants are mentioned; in 18:17b-19, the sailors.)

In heaven, however, there arises at this moment a jubilant cry of victory: "The Lord our God the Almighty reigns" (19:6) (cf. the Enthronement psalms).* With this triumphant exultation in ch. 19 the account leads over to a portrayal of the consummation in chs. 20—22.

---

*Translator's Note: For a detailed discussion of the Enthronement psalms see Mowinckel, S., *The Psalms in Israel's Worship*, Nashville: Abingdon, 1962. Vol. 1, pp. 106-189.

Now the reign of peace dawns after the terrible woes of the final age. There is to be but one last assault of Satan (20:7 ff.) and then he will be destroyed forever. The Seer continues: "Then I saw a new heaven and a new earth . . . and I saw the new Jerusalem . . . " (21:1 ff.). This new divine world will finally bring about the ultimate fulfillment of all promises—peace:

> "Behold the dwelling of God is with men.
> He will dwell with them, and they shall be his people,
> And God himself will be with them:
> he will wipe every tear from their eyes,
> and death shall be no more,
> neither shall there be mourning, nor crying, nor pain any more"
>
> (21:3-5)

It is characteristic of Revelation that this monumental portrayal of eternal salvation consists entirely of Old Testament utterances. Here for the first time the relationship of the two Testaments is completely evident. What the people of God had been promised on their long journey through history is realized for the first time through Christ's ultimate victory at the time of his return, which puts an end to the power of death and sin.

What Abraham was promised in the words: " . . . In you all the families of the earth shall be blessed" (Gen. 12:1-3) is brought to final fulfillment in the final victory of Christ. Therefore his church lives in the expectation of her Lord (22:20)—the church that is in tribulation even as she was addressed in the letters (chs. 2—3):

> "He who testifies to these things says:
> 'Surely I am coming soon.'
> Amen. Come Lord Jesus!" (22:20)

Index of Names and Subjects

Index of Scripture References

OLD TESTAMENT

NEW TESTAMENT